FAST
CARS

DRIVING THE DREAM

igloobooks

igl001books

Published in 2013
by Igloo Books Ltd
Cottage Farm
Sywell
NN6 0BJ
www.igloobooks.com

FIR003 1013
2 4 6 8 10 9 7 5 3 1
ISBN 978-1-78343-208-0

Distributed in association with G2 Entertainment Limited

Printed and manufactured in China

Contents

Introduction

▶ This 1903 60bhp Mercedes had its engine at the front driving the rear wheels. It set the tone for fast cars for years to come

What is the definition of a fast car? These days, when even a modest family saloon can drive at over 100mph, you could argue that all cars are fast. But family saloons are also rather dull. So I like to think of fast cars as those that have been designed with the sole purpose of going fast and being fun to drive.

This thinking is nothing new. When the first motorcars were preceded by a bloke with a red flag, people were already getting excited by the prospect of driving fast.

Those first rear-engined machines only chugged along at speeds of around 10mph, but by 1901, Daimler had produced a 60bhp Mercedes that was capable of 60mph and is now considered to have been the world's first sports car.

And things just got better from then onwards, with more and more manufacturers jumping on the power bandwagon.

By the 1980s, the race was on to produce a 200mph sportscar, and in 1987 Ferrari's F40 hit 201mph and the magical figure was finally broken.

As the 1990s went on, the 200mph-plus supercar became almost the norm, so McLaren had to pull out all the stops to come up with something special. And it did just that with the F1 of 1993. Not only could this reach a previously unheard of 240mph, it was also smaller, lighter and more nimble than most other supercars.

However, to reach such heady speeds cost a lot of money. Sensibly, perhaps, other manufacturers contented themselves with cars that had a top speed of close to 200mph, and concentrated

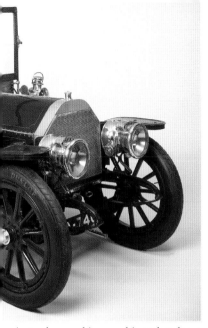

human race has always strived to improve itself. If it hadn't, we'd still be sitting in caves wondering how to make fire. And if the motorcar hadn't been allowed to develop, it would still be chugging along behind a man waving a red flag.

So, what's next? Will there ever be a road car better than the Veyron? A car capable of even greater speeds? I sincerely hope so, because it will be a sad day, indeed, when mankind stops pushing the boundaries yet further. And, remember, the benefits of producing ultra-fast cars have always filtered down into more mainstream machinery. Which is why the humble family saloon can now drive at over 100mph.

So, fast cars are an important part of our lives. Over the following pages are sixty of some of the most interesting, influential and exciting cars which were built for the sole purpose of going at high speed. It's very much a personal choice – I could easily have included twice the number – and I'm sorry if your personal favourite isn't there. Enjoy!

instead on making machines that drove and handled superbly at rather more realistic speeds.

Until, that is, the Bugatti Veyron came along. With 1000bhp on tap, this had a top speed of no less than 253mph and a 0-60mph time of just 2.9 seconds – less than the time it took you to read this sentence! Of course, the critics shook their heads, asking what was the use of producing a car capable of such speeds, when most countries don't even allow you to drive at 100mph.

But that is missing the point. The

Philip Raby

Aston Martin DB5

1964 United Kingdom

HOW TO SPOT

Smooth two-door coupe with headlamps behind streamlined plastic cowls. Long rear overhang, and traditional Aston Martin grille and side strakes.

The Aston Martin DB5 is one of the most famous cars of all time – for the simple reason Sean Connery, as James Bond, drove one in the films Goldfinger and Thunderball, in the early 1960s.

Author Ian Fleming had Bond driving an earlier DB MkIII in the novel of Goldfinger, but when the film makers approached Aston Martin for a car, they were offered the prototype of the about-to-be-released DB5, and so a legend was born.

The DB5 was an evolution of the essentially similar DB4, but with covered headlamps (although these did appear briefly on the DB4 Vantage), a more powerful 4.0-litre engine and – on all but the very early examples – a five-speed gearbox.

The straight-six engine was endowed

▼ The DB5 in rare drophead form was a seriously good-looking car

6

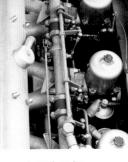

with three SU carburettors and produced 282bhp – enough to propel the car to a top speed of 148mph. However, a rare and more powerful Vantage version was fed by triple Webers and pumped out no less than 314bhp. Also rare was a soft-top version which, unlike some Astons, was not badged Volante. The rarest DB5 of all, though, was a shooting brake version built for company boss David Brown to carry his dogs in!

The James Bond car came with many unique extras, including front and rear rams, machine guns, tyre slashers, bulletproof screen, radar and telephone, smoke screen, revolving numberplates and – not least – a passenger ejector seat.

SPECIFICATION

Capacity: 3995cc
Cylinders: straight-six
Compression ratio: 8.0:1
Maximum power: 282bhp at 5500rpm
Maximum torque: 390Nm at 3850rpm
Gearbox: Five-speed manual
Length: 4572mm
Width: 1676mm
Weight: 1564kg
0-60mph: 8.6 seconds
Maximum speed: 142mph

The films gave Aston Martin excellent publicity and made the DB5 the car that young boys and grown men alike aspired to own. Bond was cool, so Astons were cool. Indeed, the effects of those early films remains to this day; surely anyone who buys an Aston Martin, if they're honest, must have been influenced by the James Bond connection.

Of course, 'real' DB5s didn't have such exotic accessories and, even putting aside the Bond connection, it was a seriously good-looking car with breathtaking performance for its time.

However, even though it's the most famous of all Aston Martins, the DB5 was in production for only two years, during which time around 1000 examples were built, with just 65 of them being the more powerful Vantage variant. Its replacement was the DB6 of 1966, which had a number of improvements, the most noticeable being a squared-off tail to improve the aerodynamics. The DB6 was built until 1971.

The DB5's 4.0-litre, straight-six engine. Note the three SU carburettors

Aston Martin Lagonda

1978 United Kingdom

In the 1970s, if you wanted a large, luxury car you bought a staid and regal Rolls Royce. But then Aston Martin came up with a radical alternative – the Lagonda was like nothing else on the road.

Designed by William Towns, the Lagonda had razor-sharp lines, with Towns' trademark wedge shape led by a rather incongruous radiator grille. At over 17 feet long, the Lagonda was an imposing machine that turned heads wherever it went.

Just as futuristic as the exterior styling was the interior, which was way ahead of its time. Instead of conventional dials, Aston Martin chose to endow the Lagonda with an ultra modern electronic dashboard with LED displays and touch-sensitive switches. More traditional were the plush leather seats and walnut trim.

Under the pointed bonnet of the Lagonda lay a rather less than

▼ The Lagonda's angular lines are like nothing else on the road

▲ In 1978 this all-black dash with touch-sensitive switches was positively space age!

HOW TO SPOT

Large, low, four-door saloon with very angular, thrust-back, wedge-shaped styling and small radiator grille on nose. Pop-up headlamps on early cars; six fixed lights on later models.

hi-tech engine. The 5.3-litre V8 was Aston's own unit and was linked to a relatively simple three-speed automatic transmission driving the rear wheels.

Unfortunately, the Lagonda's electronics were to prove troublesome and, over the years, Aston Martin made changes. The original LED instruments were replaced in 1984 with three mini cathode ray tubes (essentially tiny television screens) which displayed speed, revs and other information. This was backed up with voice messages in a choice of languages (the Lagonda was popular in Arabic countries). In 1987 these screens gave way to vacuum fluorescent read-outs.

The car's appearance was updated over the years, too. In 1987, the original sharp lines were softened – under the watchful eye of William Towns, the original designer – to drag the car some way out of the 1970s. At the same time, the pop-up headlamps – also very much of their time – were replaced by an impressive array of six fixed headlamps in the snout.

The Aston Martin Lagonda was one of the most striking cars ever made, and a tribute to 1970s design. It was, though, very expensive, sometimes unreliable and somewhat quirky. When production ended in 1989, just 645 examples were built, with about a quarter of those remaining in the UK; making the Lagonda a very rare car today.

SPECIFICATION (1987)

Capacity: 5340cc
Cylinders: V8
Compression ratio: 9.5:1
Maximum power: 280bhp at 5000rpm
Maximum torque: 434Nm at 4000rpm
Gearbox: Automatic three-speed
Length: 5283mm
Width: 1791mm
Weight: 2023kg
0-60mph: 8.9 seconds
Maximum speed: 145mph

Aston Martin DB9

2004 United Kingdom

After Ford took over Aston Martin in the 1987, it produced the achingly beautiful DB7 of 1993. And when that car was due for replacement, the company did the impossible and made an even better-looking car – the DB9. Why not DB8? Because Aston's marketing department felt that name would suggest an eight-cylinder car and the DB9 had no less than 12 cylinders under the bonnet (they also argued that

▼ Inside, the DB9 is a blend of British luxury and high technology

skipping a number would show what a great leap forward the new car was…).

The engine was essentially the same as that found in the Vanquish S, which made the DB9 remarkable value, at around £50,000 less expensive.

In the DB9 the V12 developed 450bhp with a healthy 570Nm of torque at just 5000rpm, so buyers didn't feel at all short-changed. There was a choice of transmissions – a Touchtronic automatic or a conventional six-speed manual, for those who liked to be in full control

The bodywork was arguably better-looking than that of the rather aggressive-looking Vanquish, too, with a purity of line that was hard to match. The panelwork was mainly aluminium and composites, bonded together using aerospace technology to give a combination of light weight and high strength. The Volante version had a fully automatic folding roof, for luxury open-air motoring. In the event of an accident, rollbars automatically popped-up on the Volante to protect passengers.

Inside, as you'd expect of an Aston Martin, the finish was exemplary, with hand-finished leather and wood everywhere you looked.

SPECIFICATION

Capacity: 5935cc

Cylinders: V12

Compression ratio: 10.3:1

Maximum power: 450bhp at 6000rpm

Maximum torque: 570Nm at 5000rpm

Gearbox: Automatic or six-speed manual

Length: 4710mm

Width: 1875mm

Weight: 1800kg

0-60mph: 4.9 seconds

Maximum speed: 186mph

The instruments and door handles were aluminium, while the starter button was made from crystal-clear glass. The DB7 was criticised for its Ford-sourced switchgear, but you could find nothing of the sort in the DB9.

If you should ever get bored of the sound of that V12 engine, you could enjoy music from the built-in Linn hi-fi system, while letting the cruise control help waft you to your destination.

There was very little to fault with the DB9; it's a luxury, high-performance sports car to match the best from Germany and Italy. And it encapsulated true British values of quality and craftsmanship. What more could you want?

▲ The DB9 looks stunning from any angle

11

Aston Martin Vanquish S

2004 United Kingdom

▲ The Vanquish S is an aggressive but elegant machine

The Aston Martin Vanquish arrived in 2001 and was undoubtedly a great car. With the advent of the S version three years later, things got even better.

Under that oh-so-long bonnet lay a V12 engine that looked as beautiful as the car. In S form it produced no less than 520bhp – 60bhp more than in the standard Vanquish. And 577Nm torque made the power very accessible and easy to use. It's hard to believe that this wonderful engine was, essentially, two Ford Mondeo units end to end, developed with the help of Cosworth.

The drive was taken to the rear wheels via a high-tech six-speed transmission unit that gave a choice of manual gearchanges via finger-operated paddles on the steering column, or automatic changes. In both modes there was an optional Sports setting which held lower gears for longer to make more use of the engine's power.

Large, curvaceous coupe with long, flowing bonnet and subtly bulging wings. Trademark Aston front grille and side strakes.

The Vanquish's bodyshell was lovingly hand-built from aluminium and carbonfibre, and each car took 385 man-hours to create – compared with 202 hours for its little brother, the DB9. However, there was nothing quaint or old-fashioned about the car's construction methods. Each car started as a heat-cured aluminium bonded monocoque, which was formed from a combination of extruded and folded aluminium panels that were bonded and then riveted together. The monocoque was bonded to a nine-layer carbonfibre tunnel, which gave the Vanquish S an extremely rigid yet lightweight backbone. Onto this were then affixed hand-finished aluminium body panels.

Inside, passengers were treated to an opulent cockpit. Dominating the cabin was a leather-clad centre console that arched from the top of the facia down to the transmission tunnel. Grab handles and gearshift paddles were finished in matching cast aluminium, while the rest of the cabin was trimmed in high-quality leather, Alcantara, and Wilton carpet. The instruments were a slightly retro black-on-cream and changed to a soothing blue at night.

As Ford-owned Aston Martin moved into more mainstream cars, such as the DB9 and V8 Vantage, the handcrafted Vanquish was a reminder of how Astons used to be made. And that was something to savour; especially when it was also such a gorgeous-looking and powerful beast.

The Vanquish's cockpit is stunning. Note the paddle-shifters by the steering wheel

SPECIFICATION

Capacity: 5925cc
Cylinders: V12
Compression ratio: 10.8:1
Maximum power: 520bhp at 7000rpm
Maximum torque: 577Nm at 5800rpm
Gearbox: Manual/automatic, six-speed
Length: 4665mm
Width: 1923mm
Weight: 1875kg
0-60mph: 4.7 seconds
Maximum speed: 202mph

Audi quattro

1980 Germany

HOW TO SPOT

Angular two-door hatchback with prominent wheelarch extensions front and rear, thick rear pillars, and trademark Audi 'rings' in front grille.

The Audi quattro was revolutionary in more ways than one. First, it was the first production car with four-wheel-drive since the Jenson FF of 1966. Second, it began the transformation of Audi from a somewhat staid brand into the sporty, prestige marque it is today.

While the Jenson's transmission system was heavy and troublesome, the Audi's was lightweight and reliable, thus showing to the world that production cars could, indeed, have four-wheel-

drive. The quattro may not have been the first road car so-equipped, but it was certainly the first truly successful one, and other car manufacturers were soon jumping on the bandwagon.

The key to the success was the way the drive system worked. Instead of the usual transfer box and driveshaft, the quattro had a conventional gearbox behind the front-mounted engine. However, behind this gearbox was a small differential from which one driveshaft went to the rear

▼ The original Audi quattro, with its rally heritage, looks at home in a forest

wheels, and a second ran forward to the fronts. It was simple but effective, and endowed the Audi with exception traction in slippery conditions, enhanced the handling in the dry and helped put down the power without the wheels spinning.

That power, incidentally, came from a five-cylinder engine (an unusual configuration that Audi favoured for its smoothness over a four) which was

turbocharged to enable it to produce 200bhp. This was to be a fast as well as an innovative car.

The quattro went onto storm rallying events around the world through the early 1980s, with its drive system offering astonishing levels of grip and traction. A short wheelbase version of the quattro, called the Sport, evolved from the rally cars and went on sale in 1984, with 396bhp on tap. This stripped down coupe could reach 60mph in just 4.5 seconds and had a top speed of 155mph. It remains the ultimate road-going quattro.

The Audi quattro continued in production, albeit with many updates, until 1991. However, the name – and the technology – has lived on. Audi has become well-known for its four-wheel-drive systems and so today quattro versions of most Audi road cars are offered.

⚠ From the side, the quattro's angular lines are apparent

SPECIFICATION

Capacity: 2144cc
Cylinders: straight-five
Compression ratio: 7.0:1
Maximum power: 200bhp at 5500rpm
Maximum torque: 285Nm at 3500rpm
Gearbox: Five-speed manual
Length: 4404mm
Width: 1722mm
Weight: 1290kg
0-60mph: 7.1 seconds
Maximum speed: 137mph

Audi TT 1.8T quattro Sport

2005 Germany

The Audi TT was surely the most stylish car of the 1990s, with its Bauhaus-inspired lines and neat, squat appearance. It first appeared as a show-car in 1995 and created such a stir that Audi put it into production, with surprisingly few changes, just three years later.

In the years that followed, the TT became a style icon with fashion-

conscious drivers around the world. It was offered with a choice of engines, from 180bhp and 225bhp four-cylinders to a 250bhp V6, with four-wheel-drive standard on all but the entry-level car.

The TT's lines stood the test of time remarkably well, but ten years after it first appeared it had become relatively commonplace and was not such a fashion statement. What's more, there was

HOW TO SPOT

Small two-door coupe with distinctive styling and small curved cabin top. Wraparound front and rear lights and black-painted roof.

competition from the likes of Nissan's 350Z and Porsche's Cayman, so Audi fought back with the TT 1.8T quattro Sport.

This was essentially a more extreme version of the car; lighter and sportier than the standard TT. Power came from the standard 1.8-litre turbocharged engine, albeit tweaked to produce 240bhp rather than 225bhp. However, the extra power was helped by a worthwhile 49kg weight reduction. This was achieved by ditching the spare wheel and the rather limited rear seats and parcel shelf, and by fitting lightweight Recaro seats in the front, with a aluminium strut-brace behind.

Furthermore, the suspension was firmed up to give sharper handling, and the brakes were the larger items from the V6 version of the TT.

Externally, the Sport was identified by 18-inch, 15-spoke alloy wheels, the larger front and rear spoilers from the V6 and – most noticeably – the roof and door mirrors were painted black, which gave the car a visual transformation.

The four-cylinder Sport was more

expensive and (slightly) faster than the contemporary 3.2 V6 quattro, and offered a quite different driving style; being more of a stripped out sports car, while the V6 was more refined and dignified. It did, though, freshen up the TT while the world eagerly awaited an all-new version.

▲ The Sport's superb interior is further enhanced with racing seats and steering wheel

SPECIFICATION

Capacity: 1781cc
Cylinders: Straight four
Compression ratio: 9.5:1
Maximum power: 240bhp at 5700rpm
Maximum torque: 320Nm at 2300-5000rpm
Gearbox: Manual, six-speed
Length: 4041mm
Width: 1764mm
Weight: 1416kg
0-60mph: 5.9 seconds
Maximum speed: 155mph

Bentley R Continental
1952 United Kingdom

▲ The Continental R was regal but fast

When it was launched in 1952, the Bentley R Continental was hailed as the fastest production four-seater car in the world. And, at the time, a top speed of 115mph was quite something, when most family saloons struggled to exceed 70mph.

Much of the Bentley's performance excellence was down to its shape; it was designed, with the aid of a wind-tunnel, to be aerodynamically efficient. Downforce was not a consideration in those days, so the car was shaped to slip through the air as smoothly as possible. This led to the distinctive long, flowing tail. The rear wings were finned to help high-speed stability, while on the first cars the back wheels were covered with spats for extra efficiency. The Continental was an elegant and stately

HOW TO SPOT

Large and elegant coupe with tall Bentley grille, long bonnet, sweeping wings and smooth fastback tail between finned rear wings.

car but, at the same time, one that looked fast, even when it was standing still.

Under the smooth and lightweight skin was a Rolls Royce R-Type chassis with independent front suspension with wishbones and coil springs, and a fixed rear axle with half-elliptic springs.

The engine was an inline, 4.6-litre, six-cylinder unit with twin SU carburettors. It was based on a Rolls Royce unit, but was given a higher compression ratio and a more efficient exhaust system. The power went through a manual four-speed gearbox to the rear wheels.

Priced at £6929 in 1952, the Continental was a very expensive motorcar, but lucky buyers were treated to more than just high-speed performance. The interior was, as you'd expect of a Bentley, of the highest quality, with plenty of beautifully finished leather and walnut.

In 1954, buyers were given the option of a four-speed automatic transmission, while the engine capacity was increased to 4.9-litres. A year later, the car was lengthened slightly to accommodate a new chassis. In this form, the Continental remained in production until 1959. It was to be the last purpose-designed Bentley until the Continental R of 1991; this was then followed by the all-new Continental GT of 2003, which draws inspiration from this original Continental.

The streamlined rear with finned wings to aid stability

SPECIFICATION

Capacity: 4566cc

Cylinders: Straight-six

Compression ratio: 7.25:1

Maximum power: 178bhp at 4500rpm

Maximum torque: n/a

Gearbox: Manual, four-speed

Length: 5232mm

Width: 1778mm

Weight: 1882kg

0-60mph: 13.5 seconds

Maximum speed: 115mph

Bentley Continental GT
2003 United Kingdom

For 70 years, Bentley and Rolls Royce were produced side by side and, latterly, Bentleys were little more than rebadged Rollers. However, in 2003 Bentley was taken over by Volkswagen and finally separated from its stablemate. This led to the all-new Continental GT which harked back to the glory days of the Bentley R Continental of the early 1950s which, in its time, was the fastest four-seater car in the world. Now, Bentley could once again boast that same accolade; this time with an utterly modern car that tops 198mph.

Most cars that can get to that sort of speed are uncompromising supercars with two seats and little in the way of creature comforts. Not so the Continental GT. This was a true four-seater car with all the luxury you'd expect of a Bentley. The interior was lined with acres of leather and walnut, combined

▼ The Continental GT doing what it's best at – travelling fast

Large four-seater coupe with front wings sweeping down to meet four headlamps between smoothed-out traditional Bentley grille. Prominent rear wings and high back end.

with modern essentials such as climate control, satellite navigation, hi-fi and fully electric massaging seats. The rear passengers didn't want for anything, either, with plush, cosseting seats and their own climate control.

Comfort was further enhanced by computer-controlled air springs with adjustable dampers which could be set to Sport or Comfort mode to suit the driver's style of driving.

But the GT was about more than luxury – it was also an extremely powerful motorcar. The engine was a 6.0-litre W12 unit that produced 552bhp and 650Nm torque; the latter from as little as 1600rpm. The power was fed to all four wheels via a six-speed automatic gearbox (with fingertip manual override), and was enough to make the car hit 60mph in 4.7 seconds; which is particularly impressive when you consider that the large GT weighed a hefty 2385kg.

From the outside, the Continental GT wore its heritage in pride, but without being overly retro. Its elegant lines harked back to the glory days of the 1950s, yet the car looked muscular and purposeful. Like any Bentley, it portrayed a perfect mix of exclusivity and sporty rawness. It was a motorcar for people with class but a hint of wildness about them.

▲ The Continental GT's cockpit is opulent in only the way a Bentley can be

SPECIFICATION

Capacity: 5998cc
Cylinders: W12
Compression ratio: 9.0:1
Maximum power: 552bhp at 6100rpm
Maximum torque: 650Nm at 1600rpm
Gearbox: Automatic, six-speed
Length: 4803mm
Width: 2100mm
Weight: 2385kg
0-60mph: 4.7 seconds
Maximum speed: 198mph

BMW M1

1978 Germany

HOW TO SPOT

Sleek mid-engined coupe. Low front end features pop-up headlamps and tiny stylised BMW grille in bumper. High rear deck with louvres over.

When BMW Motorsport wanted a car that could compete in Group 5 racing, against the likes of Porsche, it turned to Lamborghini for help. The project, designated E-26, was initiated in 1976 and involved building a 850bhp Group 5 car, a similar Group 4 version with 470bhp, plus a production run of 400 de-powered road-going cars for homologation purposes.

Lamborghini and Ital Design developed a sleek, ultra-modern glassfibre body over a tubular steel chassis. Power for the road-going version came from a BMW six-cylinder engine from the then-current 635 CSi coupe. Enhanced with twin overhead camshafts and four valves per cylinder, this engine produced 277bhp; 66bhp more than in the 635. Racing versions were turbocharged to produce more power. In true supercar fashion, the engine was mid-mounted to give optimum weight distribution and thus enhance the handling. The gearbox, meanwhile, was a five-speed unit driving the rear wheels.

Unfortunately, problems at Lamborghini led to delays and, eventually, BMW moved assembly to Baur in Germany, with its own Motorsport division finishing the cars.

▼ The M1 had a louvred rear deck, but still gave reasonable rear-view visibility

The M1 was finally launched in 1978, however, this was later than planned and, by this time, Group 5 rules had changed so the car was no longer viable and, besides, BMW had not sold enough road-going examples for homologation. Instead, then, the M1 raced with some success in the new

SPECIFICATION

Capacity: 3453cc

Cylinders: Straight-six

Compression ratio: 9.1:1

Maximum power: 277bhp at 6500rpm

Maximum torque: 329Nm at 5000rpm

Gearbox: Manual, five-speed

Length: 4346mm

Width: 1823mm

Weight: 1440kg

0-60mph: 5.6 seconds

Maximum speed: 162mph

Procar series until production ceased in 1981.

As a road car, the M1 excelled. It offered excellent performance and handling combined with BMW's usual reliability and build quality, plus relatively low running costs. The two-seater cockpit was very BMW-like and, as such, was functional and comfortable, with full carpets, leather and air-conditioning.

The M1 was undoubtedly a great car, and a worthy competitor to often less-reliable supercars from other manufacturers. Sadly, though, in total, just 455 examples were built, of which 399 were road-worthy, making it an extremely rare collector's item today. Famously, artist Andy Warhol hand-painted a racing M1 in 1979, as part of BMW's 'Art Cars' programme.

▲ The M1 supercar was like no BMW before – or since

Bugatti Veyron 16.4

2005 France

HOW TO SPOT

Large, sleek two-seater coupe, with scooped side intakes, swooping bonnet leading to Bugatti front grille, square exhaust tailpipe and retractable rear wing.

There are supercars and there is the Bugatti Veyron 16.4. When Volkswagen decided, in 1998, to resurrect the famous Bugatti name it didn't hold anything back. The Veyron redefined the term supercar with power and torque figures unlike anything that has come before it.

Let's cut straight to the chase. The Veyron mid-mounted engine produced over 1000bhp. Actually, the official VW figure was 'only' 987bhp, but in reality the output was believed to be closer to 1035bhp. Indeed, an indicator on the dash let you know when the power reached the magic four-figure number (if you dared look because you were likely to be travelling at over 200mph

▼ The Veyron has a retractable rear spoiler to give extra downforce at high speed

when this happened…). But perhaps even more impressive was the engine's torque figure of 922lb ft or 1250Nm; that's almost double the figure of the McLaren F1.

Those impressive figures came courtesy of an impressive engine, with no less than 16 cylinders arranged in a 'W' configuration (essentially, two V8s joined at the crankshaft). The capacity was a hearty 8.3-litres and the cylinders were fed by no less than four turbochargers. And to keep it all cool, there were ten – yes, ten – radiators and two independent cooling circuits.

The power was fed to all four wheels through a seven-speed gearbox with the option of automatic or manual shifts, the latter courtesy of steering wheel-mounted paddles. And the power was then harnessed back by a set of massive ceramic disc brakes.

All this technology was clothed in an astonishingly beautiful body hand-made from carbonfibre and aluminium. It was undoubtedly a modern car, yet the designers managed to incorporate some of the old Bugatti charm into its lines;

not least with the evocative radiator grille and badge. And, of course, the shape was defined by aerodynamic requirements to ensure that the car remained firmly on the roads at speeds up to over 250mph.

Inside, the Veyron was pure luxury, with no plastic to be seen anywhere.

SPECIFICATION

Capacity: 8.3-litre
Cylinders: W16
Compression ratio: 9.0:1
Maximum power: 987bhp at 6000rpm
Maximum torque: 1250Nm at 2200-5500rpm
Gearbox: Semi-automatic, six-speed
Length: 4380mm
Width: 1994mm
Weight: 1888kg
0-60mph: 2.9 seconds
Maximum speed: 253mph

Instead, you found leather and aluminium, all lovingly hand-crafted. Even the hi-fi unit had bespoke aluminium controls.

Incidentally, the Veyron was named after the French racing driver, Pierre Veyron, who won the 1939 Le Mans race in a 57C Bugatti.

The top speed of the Veyron was limited – if that's the right word – to 253mph because the tyres were not considered capable of faster speeds. No one knows what the car was truly capable of. Combined with a price tag in 2005 of $1-million (around £840,000), these are yet more figures that help to define the Bugatti Veyron as the supercar to beat all supercars. Surely, in these politically correct days, no one will ever have the tenacity to produce a more outrageous machine.

The fastest car on the planet. And it looks it!

Caterham Seven CSR260

2006 United Kingdom

Way back in 1957, a new sports car was unveiled that was to become an enduring legend. It was the Lotus Seven; a simple two-seater car for track and road use, that you built yourself from a kit of parts.

Over the years, the little Lotus became a firm favourite with drivers looking for an affordable and fun car, and the model was refined with more power and sophistication, while retaining the classic appearance. It gathered a cult following after it was featured heavily in the introduction of the 1960s television

series, The Prisoner.

However, by 1973 Lotus was more interested in its upcoming and upmarket Esprit and Elite models, so it passed the rights to build the Seven on to Caterham Cars, which was previously an agent for Lotus.

The car was renamed the Caterham Seven and continued to go from strength to strength, with a number of redesigns over the years to keep it competitive.

The Caterham CSR260 appeared in 2006, and was claimed to be 85

▼ The CSR260 gives ultimate driving thrills

HOW TO SPOT

Tiny, open two-seater with front 'cycle wings' that turn with the wheels. Wide rear wings covering 10-inch wide wheels. Simple side-screens and hood.

percent new and the fastest production Seven to date. Under the tiny bonnet was shoehorned a 2.3-litre Cosworth-developed all-alloy, 16-valve Ford engine that produces 260bhp. In the small and lightweight aluminium and glassfibre Seven, this gave crazy performance, with a top speed of 155mph and a 0-60mph time of just 3.1 seconds. This made it one of the world's fastest accelerating cars – beating even the McLaren F1 and only a fraction behind the Bugatti Veyron, which cost more than 20 times the price of the little Caterham!

An all-new, Formula 1 style fully independent suspension system, front and rear, combined with 10-inch wide rear wheels, ensured that the CSR260 handled as well as it accelerates. And a six-speed gearbox let you make the best use of the power.

No Caterham is luxurious, but the CSR made some concessions to passenger comfort in the form of a new curved dash with novel exposed steel tubing, carpets and even some storage space.

The CSR260 was a frighteningly fast car – there are few that could beat it from A to B on the public roads – and not one for the faint-hearted. However, Caterham still produces a range of less-extreme Sevens, including some you can still build yourself; which really is in the spirit of the original Lotus all those years ago.

▲ The CSR260 has a small but perfectly formed cockpit. Note the exposed tubework

SPECIFICATION

Capacity: 2261cc
Cylinders: Straight-four
Compression ratio: 12:1
Maximum power: 260bhp at 7500rpm
Maximum torque: 271Nm at 6200rpm
Gearbox: Six-speed manual
Length: 3300mm
Width: 1685mm
Weight: n/a
0-60mph: 3.1 seconds
Maximum speed: 155mph

Chevrolet Corvette Sting Ray

1963 USA

In the early 1950s, Americans were increasingly buying open-top British sports cars, so in 1953 General Motors hit back with the Chevrolet Corvette.

However, it was the Corvette Sting Ray a decade later that really made the model a legend. Here was a car which looked quite stunning with its long bonnet, flowing wings and fast-back rear with

▼ The Corvette Stingray was a true American supercar. This is a 1967 drophead

a distinctive split back window. Like earlier (and all subsequent) Corvettes, the body was made of glassfibre, which afforded the designers the freedom to be extra adventurous with the car's lines.

Inspired by Britain's E-type Jaguar, the Sting Ray looked fast from every angle, and is still remembered as the definitive Corvette that all later ones try to emulate. An open-top roadster

HOW TO SPOT

Distinctive coupe with 'Coke bottle' lines,
long bonnet with concealed headlamps,
split rear window (on early cars) and four
round rear lamps.

version looked pretty but lacked the ultimate outrageousness of the coupe.

Under that long, sleek bonnet lurked a 5.4-litre (or 327cid in US-speak) V8 engine that initially produced 250bhp – a very respectable figure in 1963. However, over the years the engine was upgraded to as much as 435bhp.

The power was fed through a relatively simple two-speed automatic or a three-speed manual transmission. Luckily, the torquey engine almost negated the need for more gear ratios, although a four-speed manual was an option.

The Sting Ray was a fast car, even in 250bhp form, with 60mph coming up in just 5.9 seconds and the top speed was 142mph. However, the soft leaf-sprung independent suspension and all-round drum brakes on the first examples (thankfully, discs arrived in 1965) meant that the car didn't have the handling or stopping capabilities to match its power!

A year after the car's introduction, the split rear window was replaced by a single-piece item to improve visibility. However, to this day, the early Sting Rays are the most sought after for the simple reason that the split window looks so good.

Now known as a second-generation or C2 Corvette, this Sting Ray was discontinued in 1967, to be replaced by a larger, more powerful car. However, these early Sting Ray remain the most striking and memorable of all Corvettes. They really are the true American supercar.

▲ Under the bonnet lay a small-block V8 engine

SPECIFICATION

Capacity: 5300cc
Cylinders: V8
Compression ratio: 10.5:1
Maximum power: 250bhp at 4400rpm
Maximum torque: 474Nm at 2800rpm
Gearbox: Two-speed automatic or three-speed manual
Length: 4450mm
Width: 1758mm
Weight: 1424kg
0-60mph: 5.9 seconds
Maximum speed: 142mph

Chevrolet Corvette Z06

2006 USA

▲ The Z06 is the ultimate road-going incarnation of the Corvette

The Americans have always lagged behind Europe when it comes to supercars, but the Corvette Z06 was designed to give Porsche and Ferrari a run for their money. Indeed, in 2006 it was the fastest car Chevrolet had ever built, with a top speed of 190mph.

In 2004 the company had a successful year with the Corvette C5-R racecar, so it decided to apply some of that car's technology to a road vehicle. And the Z06 was the result.

Based on the standard Corvette, the Z06 had a massive 7.0-litre V8 engine that produced 505bhp and a serious 637Nm of torque. The engine covers were painted bright red to distinguish it from lesser powerplants.

Unlike other Corvettes, which could be bought with an automatic transmission, the Z06 was only available with a six-speed manual

Sleek, low coupe with scalloped sides, air intakes in wings and high rear end. Distinctive slanted headlamps and trademark Corvette round rear lights.

gearbox, driving the rear wheels.

Visually, the Z06 was similar to the rest of the Corvette family, but with the addition of vents in the front and rear wings, a deeper front spoiler and a small bonnet scoop to feed air to the engine. The wings were slightly wider front and rear, too, and there was a small ducktail spoiler to aid aerodynamics. Unlike the other models, the Z06's roof panel was fixed in place to save weight and increase body stiffness.

The body, by the way, was made of glassfibre and carbonfibre and mounted on a lightweight aluminium chassis.

Despite its racecar heritage, the Z06 had a highly specced interior with supportive, two-tone leather-clad sports seats (with 'Z06' logos on the headrests), and even included cupholders. An interesting feature was a head-up display that projected your speed, engine revs and G-force up in front of your face. It was similar to the technology used in modern fighter jets.

The Corvette Z06 was an odd mix of traditional Yank muscle car (the

engine used old-fashioned pushrods). It may not have had the finesse or quality of a European supercar, but it sure made up for it in terms of sheer grunt and road presence.

From behind, the Z06 has the trademark Corvette round lights – there's no mistaking what it is

SPECIFICATION

Capacity: 6998cc
Cylinders: V8
Compression ratio: 11.1:1
Maximum power: 505bhp at 6300rpm
Maximum torque: 637Nm at 4800rpm
Gearbox: Six-speed manual
Length: 4460mm
Width: 1928mm
Weight: 1421kg
0-60mph: 3.7 seconds
Maximum speed: 190mph

Dare DZ

1998 United Kingdom

HOW TO SPOT

Tiny, two-seater with low, pointed snout with small fins on each side and separate front 'cycle wings'. Retractable headlamps below windscreen. Bulbous rear with side air intakes. Gullwing doors on coupe.

The British have always been good at building small, fun sports cars and the Dare DZ was no exception. The distinctive car was the brainchild of the Walklett brothers who previously produced the Ginetta range of cars from the 1950s to the 1980s.

The little mid-engined DZ first appeared in 1998 and immediately appealed to enthusiasts who wanted a lightweight, mid-engined car that would, above everything else, be a lot of fun to drive.

And the DZ was certainly that. Power came from a transverse-mounted Ford Zetec 2.0-litre engine that produced 130bhp in conventional form, or a heady 210bhp when supercharged. In a car that weighed just 680kg, that made for very lively performance, with 60mph coming up in 4.7 seconds in the supercharged car, followed by a top speed of 145mph.

The mid-mounted engine ensured a 50:50 weight distribution which, combined with all-round fully independent wishbone suspension, meant that the DZ handled like a racecar, with no need for any form of driver aids; not even power steering.

The wasp-like body was available in both open and closed forms. The open car had a tiny removable hood, while the coupe had a very curved roof with gullwing doors. A clever feature were the headlamps, which were neat retractable units that popped out from each side of the body, just below the curved windscreen. The bodyshell was glassfibre and mounted on a light but

▼ The DZ's interior is small but surprisingly well-equipped

strong tubular-steel chassis.

The DZ's interior was small but surprisingly well-appointed, with leather seats, race harnesses and a comprehensive range of instruments in a leather-clad dash. It had carpets and a full heating and ventilation system, and there was even a small but useful boot space behind the engine.

The Dare DZ was built in very small numbers but proved popular with people looking for a mid-mounted and modern alternative to, say, a Caterham.

▲ The Dare DZ is an intriguing mix of old and modern. It's like nothing else on the road

SPECIFICATION

Capacity: 1996cc

Cylinders: Straight-four

Compression ratio: 10:1

Maximum power: 210bhp at 5750rpm

Maximum torque: 254Nm at 4250rpm

Gearbox: Five-speed manual

Length: 3470mm

Width: 1650mm

Weight: 680kg

0-60mph: 4.7 seconds

Maximum speed: 145mph

De Tomaso Pantera

1970 Italy

Born in Argentina, Alejandro DE Tomaso founded his automobile company in Modena, Italy, in 1959. At first, it built racing cars and limited-production sports cars but then, in 1970, it unveiled its first real production car – the Pantera (which is Italian for panther). And what a car it was!

The Pantera was developed in co-operation with Ford, USA, which wanted an affordable mid-engined supercar. To this end, the car was powered by a 5.7-litre Ford V8 engine. This developed 310bhp and, following the example set by the Lamborghini Muira, it was mounted amidships, to ensure a perfect weight distribution front and rear. Unlike the Muira, though, the V8 was mounted longitudinally, with a five-speed

▼ This 1974 Pantera looks wilder than ever in bright yellow

gearbox driving the rear wheels. Performance was good, with 60mph coming up in just 5.5 seconds, and the top speed hitting 159mph.

The bodywork was styled by Ghia and was an all-steel monocoque which gave a relatively light and strong structure for a reasonably low cost. Interestingly, though, in 1989 the car was redesigned with a separate tubular chassis.

The first Panteras were sold in the USA through Ford's Lincoln and Mercury dealers and were competitively priced at 'around $10,000', to quote the advertising of the day. However, these early cars suffered reliability problems and, for this and other reasons, Ford withdrew from

its partnership with De Tomaso in 1973, after 6128 cars had been sold. However, that was not the end of the Pantera – far from it.

De Tomaso moved to smaller premises and continued to build the Pantera, albeit in much smaller quantities and at a higher price. Indeed, over the next 17 years only about another 1000 examples were built, and it was no longer sold in the USA.

The Pantera was, though, developed over the years. The GTS model of 1973 had a 350bhp engine, while GT4 version had a 500bhp 5.7-litre and was, essentially, a racecar for the road. Indeed, in the 1970s the Pantera proved itself as a successful racer at events such as Le Mans.

The final incarnation came in 1989 when the body was redesigned with the aforementioned tubular chassis and updated, more aggressive, lines. The last Pantera was built in 1993, to be replaced by the Guara.

▲ Inside, the Pantera was an odd mix – note the vertically-mounted radio!

SPECIFICATION (1971)

Capacity: 5763cc

Cylinders: V8

Compression ratio: 11.0:1

Maximum power: 310bhp at 5400rpm

Maximum torque: 481Nm at 4000rpm

Gearbox: Manual, five-speed

Length: 4242mm

Width: 1701mm

Weight: 1416g

0-60mph: 5.5 seconds

Maximum speed: 159mph

De Lorean DMC-12
1981 United Kingdom

When American engineer and automobile executive, John De Lorean, decided to build his own sports car he ended up creating a scandal and a motoring legend at the same time. De Lorean had a vision of an 'ethical sports car' and began planning it in the mid-1970s, using some radical engineering solutions. However, these turned out to be impractical and the car had to be redesigned with the help of Lotus, which meant it ended up with much the same chassis and suspension as the Lotus Esprit.

However, the Giugiaro-designed body with its distinctive gullwing doors remained. The most striking aspect of the body was its unpainted stainless-steel cladding, which meant that minor scratches could easily be removed.

▶ The De Lorean certainly looked futuristic with its stainless-steel bodywork and gullwing doors

Low and wide coupe with angular lines, four square headlamps, gullwing doors and unique stainless-steel finish.

Underneath this was a Renault-built 2.8-litre V6 engine that produced 130bhp (it was heavily restricted for the USA market). This was a good unit, but not powerful enough to enable the De Lorean to compete with similarly priced offerings from the likes of Porsche. The handling, too, was compromised from Lotus's original configuration, because the ride height had to be raised for US regulations.

To try and keep costs down, De Lorean chose to build his car in Northern Ireland, which at the time had high unemployment so the British Government gave him a large grant to get the factory established, despite warnings from industry experts that the project was unlikely to succeed. However, even government help wasn't enough to make the De Lorean succeed. The cars were plagued with problems, due to poor development and an inexperienced workforce, and production was intermittent. And then, in 1982, John De Lorean was arrested for selling cocaine and the company finally went into liquidation shortly afterwards. Less than 9000 cars were built.

The De Lorean story is one of countless mistakes, but it's also a story of one man's vision to build an all-new sports car. And the De Lorean could have been so much more, if only things had turned out differently. As it was, the De Lorean was guaranteed immortality after appearing in the Back to the Future films of the 1980s. Let's face it, what other car travels in time once it reaches 88mph?

The interior was less radical, and you could have been in any car of the period

Capacity: 2849cc
Cylinders: V6
Compression ratio: 8.8:1
Maximum power: 130bhp at 5500rpm
Maximum torque: 208Nm at 2750rpm
Gearbox: Five-speed manual or three-speed automatic
Length: 4267mm
Width: 1988mm
Weight: 1233kg
0-60mph: 10.1 seconds
Maximum speed: 110mph

Dodge Viper SRT10

2003 USA

▲ There's no doubt that the Viper is a mean and aggressive-looking car, from any angle

When Dodge showed the original Viper concept car in 1989, it created a storm. In 1992, the production roadster went on sale, followed a year later by a coupe version. Americans were delighted – here was a true Yank muscle car with power and handling to match its looks.

The first Vipers were powered by a Lamborghini-developed 8.0-litre V10 engine that developed 400bhp and, in true American fashion, was front-mounted and drove the rear wheels. Interestingly, the engine was based on an iron truck unit that was revamped in aluminium; yet it still retained its antiquated pushrod, two valves per cylinder design. This was an engine that relied on capacity, not sophistication, for its power! The simple approach continued with the glassfibre body on

Aggressive-looking two seater. Long bonnet with air intake and slanted headlamp units with large driving lights below. Massive vents behind front wheels. Exhausts exit from side sills.

a steel tubular frame, while there were no driver aids such as ABS or traction control.

The Viper was a great success and was followed by more powerful versions, including the lightweight GTS-R racecar which had a 700bhp engine and finished first and second in class at Le Mans in 1998.

In 2003, a new Viper was introduced. Called the SRT-10, this had a heavily restyled body which was more angular and even more aggressive than the original. The engine was enlarged to 8.3-litre, which increased power to 500bhp and torque to 711Nm. In fact, in American-speak, this equated to 500ci capacity, 500bhp of power, and 500lb ft of torque – three 500s!

The new Viper had more sophisticated suspension and brakes (with ABS this time) and was a competent performer on road and track. Performance was better than ever, with a top speed of 190mph and a 0-60mph time of just 3.9 seconds. Not bad for a truck engine!

In fact, the same engine has been installed into a Dodge Ram SRT-10 truck and – bizarrely – into a motorcycle! That's right, the Dodge Tomahawk was little more than an engine with a wheel at each end. Although ten examples were sold as 'rolling sculptures' to show off the V10 engine it could, in theory, be ridden; with an estimated 0-60mph time of just 2.5 seconds and a top speed of over 300mph! And you thought the Viper was mad!

Under the Viper's long bonnet lurks a powerful V10 engine

SPECIFICATION

Capacity: 8300cc
Cylinders: V10
Compression ratio: 9.6:1
Maximum power: 500bhp at 5600rpm
Maximum torque: 711Nm at 4100rpm
Gearbox: Six-speed manual
Length: 4445mm
Width: 1911mm
Weight: 1533kg
0-60mph: 3.9 seconds
Maximum speed: 190mph

Ferrari 250 GTO

1962 Italy

HOW TO SPOT

Curvaceous coupe with long, low bonnet and cockpit thrust back. Twin vertical 'gills' in each front wing. Three half-round intakes in the nose, with an oval intake below. Large air vents behind the rear wheels.

The legendary 250 GTO is one of the most sought-after sports cars, not to mention Ferraris, of all time. And for good reason, too. Just 39 are believed to have been built, essentially for use in sport car racing events – GTO stands for 'Grand Turismo Omologato' or 'Grand Touring Homologated'. Homologated essentially means approved for racing. Actually, racing rules stipulated that 100 examples of a model be built for it to qualify, but Enzo Ferrari somehow overcame that technicality, arguing that it was based on an older model.

It was, in fact, developed from the 250 GT, and the GTO's flowing lines were developed with the help of a wind tunnel, and was one of the first road cars to have a rear spoiler to aid aerodynamics. Of course, it also had more than a dash of Italian flair drawn into its styling, and the GTO must surely be one of the best-looking cars of all time.

Under that long bonnet sat a 3-litre, V12 engine that developed 295bhp – an astonishing amount in the early 1960s. A handful of cars were fitted with even more powerful 4-litre engines. Even the standard engine, though, was enough to propel the GTO to a top speed of 185mph. A dry-sump lubrication system enabled the engine to sit low in the car to reduce the centre of gravity. The engine was fed by a mouth-watering array of six Weber 38DCN twin carburettors, and had just two valves per cylinders. The block and cylinder heads were made of alloy.

Unfortunately, the car's suspension didn't really do the immense power justice. For homologation purposes, it had to have the live rear axle and leaf springs of the older GT. At the front, though, there was a more sophisticated

▼ The 250 GTO is surely one of the most beautiful cars ever

40

A GTO where it's most at home – on a racetrack

independent wishbone system.

That said, the 250 GTO was a formidable machine on the racetrack and with it Ferrari won the 3-litre GT World Championship in 1962, 1963 and 1964. One also came second at Le Mans in 1962. In addition, GTOs triumphed at a range of other races around the world.

This race history, the prancing horse badge, the car's rarity and its drop-dead-gorgeous lines, all combined to make the 250 GTO the coveted machine it is today, with the few examples there are changing hands for immense sums of money.

SPECIFICATION

Capacity: 2953cc

Cylinders: V12

Compression ratio: 9.8:1

Maximum power: 290bhp at 7400rpm

Maximum torque: 339Nm at 8000rpm

Gearbox: Manual, five-speed

Length: 4325mm

Width: 1600mm

Weight: 1060kg

0-60mph: 5.8 seconds

Maximum speed: 185mph

Ferrari Testarossa

1984 Italy

HOW TO SPOT

Wide, low car with distinctive fined side-intakes, with the waistline curving up into the rear wings. Back lights hidden behind full-width grille.

When the Testarossa appeared in 1984 it was the world's fastest production car, with a top speed of 180mph, making it a fitting replacement for the Berlinetta Boxer.

It was planned to be, not only supremely fast, but also luxurious and comfortable for long-distance cruising. This was no stripped out racer.

Like the Boxer, the Testarossa had a horizontally opposed 12-cylinder engine, although this was an all-new 4942cc

▼ The Testarossa's side profile, with those massive strakes, was unmistakeable

unit that had little in common with its predecessor. Producing 390bhp, it didn't use any form of forced induction, relying instead on good old-fashioned capacity for its power, that pushed the car to 60mph in 5.6 seconds. The engine's red-painted cam covers gave the car its evocative name – 'red head'.

The engine was cooled by twin radiators mounted on each side of the car, in front of the rear wheels. And this led to the Testarossa's most distinctive

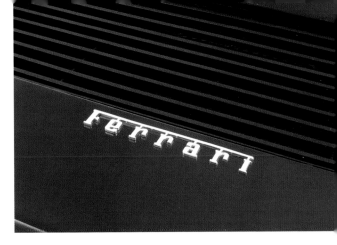

features – its immense width and those air intakes. The car had to be wide at the back to accommodate the big engine, and sticking a radiator on each side, meant it ended up being the widest car of its time, at no less than 1976mm from flank to flank.

The finned air intakes were unmistakeable and helped direct air to the radiators, but their main purpose was surely to give the Testarossa an aggressive and purposeful side view. Whatever way you looked at it, this was one mean-looking car, with its oh-so-wide flanks, low bonnet, pop-up headlamps and rear lamps concealed menacingly behind a full-width grille.

SPECIFICATION

Capacity: 4942cc
Cylinders: flat-12
Compression ratio: 9.0:1
Maximum power: 390bhp at 6300rpm
Maximum torque: 480Nm at 4500pm
Gearbox: Manual, five-speed
Length: 4486mm
Width: 1976mm
Weight: 1506kg
0-60mph: 5.6 seconds
Maximum speed: 180mph

▲ One of the most evocative badges in motoring

Inside, occupants were treated to a pair of electrically-adjustable, leather-trimmed seats, with some handy luggage space behind (special leather bags were offered that made the best use of this, and the front boot, area). Many of the controls were positioned between the seats in the centre console, alongside the slender gearstick in its traditional Ferrari 'gate'.

In 1991, the Testarossa evolved into the 512TR and then, in 1995, into the F512M. With each evolution, the car's styling and performance were enhanced to keep it up to date.

To some, the Testarossa looks dated these days, but to others it is the epitome of supercar cool, and the subject of many a schoolboy's poster.

Ferrari F40

1987 Italy

HOW TO SPOT

Angular, slightly wedged styling, twin triangular air intakes on each side, front wings extending beyond the doors in width, massive rear wing.

The F40 was produced in 1987 to celebrate 40 years of Ferrari car production; hence the name. It was also a response to Porsche's world-beating 959.

Ferrari wanted a car that would eclipse Porsche's glory, and the F40 did just that. With a top speed of 201mph it was, at the time, the world's fastest production car.

It was, though, quite different to the

▼ The F40 has a no-nonsense shape designed for speed. Count those air intakes!

hi-tech and complex 959. The F40 was very much a no-frills racecar for the road with none of the Porsche's sophisticated drivetrain and electronics.

Instead, the F40 gained its advantages by being lightweight and simple. Extensive use of Kevlar and carbonfibre in the bodyshell, and the elimination of any unnecessary 'luxuries', helped ensure that the Ferrari weighed just 1100kg

(the 959, in comparison, was a portly 1650kg).

This, combined with a 478bhp engine, ensured the Italian car's dominance. The alloy V8, which was derived from the GTO's unit, had a capacity of just 3-litres but careful design, combined with four valves per cylinder and twin turbochargers, gave the incredible output. And if that wasn't enough, buyers could opt for power upgrades of up to 200bhp!

The F40's styling was derived from that of the GTO, but designed with aerodynamic stability in mind, with a low front, smooth undertray and a large rear spoiler.

SPECIFICATION

Capacity: 2936cc

Cylinders: V8

Compression ratio: 7.7:1

Maximum power: 478bhp at 7000rpm

Maximum torque: 577Nm at 4000rpm

Gearbox: Manual, five-speed

Length: 4430mm

Width: 1980mm

Weight: 1100kg

0-60mph: 4.8 seconds

Maximum speed: 201mph

▲ Lift the F40's lightweight rear end for access to the engine, suspension and exhaust system

NACA-style ducts on each side of the car fed the turbochargers and cooling system, while louvres on the plastic rear window further helped the engine to dissipate heat.

Inside, there was little in the way of luxuries, with no carpet, no provision for a stereo (not that you'd hear one), while the door releases were simple cords, and the windows sliding plastic panels. Occupants were held in place by lightweight Kevlar racing seats and harnesses. This was very much a car for use on the track, not for long road journeys; although there was a surprisingly spacious luggage compartment at the front.

Not only was the F40's top-speed world-beating, the car could also get there quickly; with 60mph coming up in 4.8 seconds, and 124mph in just 12 seconds. This was a pure driver's car; but only for those drivers with the skill and confidence to tame such a phenomenal beast.

Ferrari F50

1995 Italy

HOW TO SPOT

Low and wide with cab thrust forward.
Distinctive black 'gap' down each side of
the bodywork, deep scoops in the front
engine, and large, integral rear wing.

The F40 arrived in 1987 to celebrate Ferrari's 40th birthday that year, but its successor, the F50, came two years early, in 1995, and is an even faster car.

Like the F40, the F50 was essentially a lightweight racer for the road, with a carbonfibre bodyshell. Under this was a chassis – also carbonfibre – which, unusually, was integral with the mid-mounted engine. In other words, the front part of the chassis was attached to the front of the engine, and the rear part to the back of the engine, so that the engine actually formed part of the chassis. This saved weight, but did mean that more engine noise was transmitted into the cockpit, because there were no isolating engine mounts.

The engine itself, unlike the F40's, was not turbocharged. Instead, it was

▼ The F50's beautifully sleek lines look especially good in red

▲ Much of the F50's bodywork was made of lightweight carbonfibre

a naturally aspired V12 unit with a capacity of 4.7-litres and a power output of 513bhp, which made it the most powerful non-turbo engine of its day. Interestingly, this arrangement followed Formula 1 thinking because, in the days of the F40, Formula 1 cars were turbocharged, but in 1995 turbos were banned by F1 in favour of larger capacity normally aspired engines.

The power went to the rear wheels via a six-speed gearbox utilising a conventional floor-mounted shift with a traditional Ferrari 'gate'. In this area, the F50 broke with Formula 1 technology, where gear changes are made electronically with finger-operated paddles.

SPECIFICATION

Capacity: 4698cc

Cylinders: V12

Compression ratio: 11.3:1

Maximum power: 513bhp at 8000rpm

Maximum torque: 470Nm at 6500rpm

Gearbox: Manual, six-speed

Length: 4480mm

Width: 1986mm

Weight: 1230kg

0-60mph: 3.7 seconds

Maximum speed: 202mph

The F50's interior was a no-nonsense place to be, trimmed with lightweight carbonfibre and aluminium. The two dials – a speedometer and tachometer – were hi-tech liquid-crystal displays, while occupants benefit from air-conditioning (although you could argue that was a necessity in such a cramped cockpit with a V12 engine behind your head!) but very little else. For instance, there was no provision for a stereo system, which reflected the serious nature of the car as a pure driving machine (not to mention the fact the very high noise levels would render one useless). The leather-covered, lightweight racing seats were available in two sizes – large or small and had simple manual adjustment. The pedals, too, were adjustable.

The Ferrari F50 was offered in both coupe and open-top forms, and just 349 examples were built between 1995 and 1997, making it rare and sought-after car.

Ferrari Enzo

2002 Italy

HOW TO SPOT

Distinctive pointed snout with elongated headlamps each side. Wide flanks aside narrow 'bubble' cockpit. Massive rear wings with air intakes at front and quad taillamps behind.

▲ The Enzo may not be the prettiest Ferrari, but its Formula One inspired lines leave no doubt as to the car's potential

With the help of Michael Schumacher, Ferrari dominated Formula 1 in recent years, so what better way to celebrate than to produce what was essentially a racing car for the road?

The Enzo even looked a bit like a Formula 1 car, with its pointed nose and forward cab position. It may not have been the prettiest Ferrari, but this car's styling was all about function. The carbon-fibre-clad shape drewon Formula 1 aerodynamics to give ground-hugging downforce at speed, to the extent that the Enzo didn't need a large rear wing, as often found on supercars.

And good aerodynamics are essential

for a car with 660bhp on tap. The power came from a lightweight, normally aspirated, 6.0-litre V12 engine, mounted amidships. This hi-tech engine produced 519Nm of torque from as low as 3000rpm to ensure that – unlike a Formula 1 car – the Enzo was relatively easy to drive on the public roads.

The power was fed to the rear wheels only (as with a Formula 1 machine) via a six-speed sequential gearbox operated via paddle-shifters on the steering column.

With these shifters was a race-style 350mm diameter steering wheel, with a flat-top containing a row of LEDs that indicated the engine revs – yet another feature borrowed from Formula 1.

And another was the fact that each Enzo was custom-built to suit its owner. After you placed an order for one of the ultra-rare cars (only 399 were produced), you were invited to the Ferrari factory for a 'fitting'. The leather-trimmed Sparco seats were then made to suit your body size, while the accelerator and brake pedals were positioned to suit your height and driving technique.

The Enzo was named after the company's founder, Enzo Ferrari, who died in 1988 and, to date, was the fastest road car the company has ever built, with a top speed of 217mph and a 0-60mph time of just 3.65 seconds. It was car that does justice to its name, carrying on Ferrari's original tradition of building cars that are, first and foremost, exhilarating and pure to drive. The Enzo shunned unnecessary luxuries in favour of an experience which was as near as a few, very lucky people, would ever get to piloting a Formula 1 car.

▲ The Enzo's 6.0-litre V12 engine develops no less than 660bhp

SPECIFICATION

Capacity: 5998cc

Cylinders: V12

Compression ratio: 660bhp at 7800rpm

Maximum power: 657Nm at 5500rpm

Maximum torque: 657Nm at 5500rpm

Gearbox: Six-speed sequential

Length: 4702mm

Width: 2035mm

Weight: 1365kg

0-60mph: 3.6 seconds

Maximum speed: 217mph

Ferrari F430

2004 Italy

HOW TO SPOT

Two seater bodyshell with high front bumper containing two large, curved air intakes. Projector headlamps under elongated covers. Round rear lamps protrude from the back wings.

The F430 was launched in 2004 as the replacement for the 360 Modena. Although based on the out-going car, Ferrari said the F430 is 70 percent new, including the larger and more powerful engine.

▼ The F430 in open-top Spyder form with its cool transparent engine cover

That engine was a mid-mounted V8 of 4.3-litre capacity. Normally aspirated,

it produced 490bhp and the power was fed to the rear wheels via an all-new six-speed sequential gearbox. Called 'Impulse', in race mode this could make changes in as little as 150 milliseconds. The transmission had another innovation called 'E-Diff', which allowed the driver to adjust the differential to suit the conditions, choosing from snow, slippy, sport, race and disengage; the latter being a conventional limited-slip differential setting.

This and other settings were made by a knob called 'Manettino', which also adjusted the suspension and traction control, plus the change speed of the transmission.

Behind the 19-inch wheels were optional massive carbon-ceramic brake discs that provided stopping capabilities to match the power and speed of the F430 – yet another example of the high technology built into this Ferrari.

The F430's distinctive lines were designed to be aerodynamically efficient, with a flat undertray. The drag co-efficient was 0.33, while at 186mph the

car generated 280kg downforce to help pin it to the road. It perhaps was not the prettiest or the most outragcous-looking Ferrari, preferring instead to appear functional and understated.

Inside, as well as the aforementioned Manettino, the steering wheel also held the bright-red starter button, and gear-changes were made via Formula 1-style paddles on the steering column. The driver was treated to a view of a bright-yellow tachometer, while the rest of the cockpit was typically Ferrari-functional, albeit clad in high-quality leather.

The F430 was also available in open-top Spyder form. This was arguably the better-looking car, with an electrically operated hood and a transparent engine cover, so onlookers could see the pulsing heart of the car.

▲ The F430's cockpit. Note the Manettino and starter buttons on the steering wheels

Although this was the entry-level Ferrari of the early 21st century, it's interesting to note that it had more power than the wild F40 of 1987, and outperformed that car to 60mph, although the F430 just failed to hit the magic 200mph mark. But for real-world use, it had all the performance you could ever want, and was infinitely more user-friendly and practical than the F40, great as that car was.

SPECIFICATION

Capacity: 4308cc

Cylinders: V8

Compression ratio: 11.3:1

Maximum power: 490bhp at 8500rpm

Maximum torque: 465Nm at 5250rpm

Gearbox: Six-speed sequential

Length: 4512mm

Width: 1923mm

Weight: 1450kg

0-60mph: 3.9 seconds

Maximum speed: 197mph

Ford GT40

1964 United Kingdom

HOW TO SPOT

Low and taut mid-engined sports coupe with very curved windscreen, cowled headlamps, triangular air intakes in bonnet, and further intakes in the rear wings.

The Ford GT40 was developed solely because Henry Ford II wanted a car that would win the Le Mans 24-hour race. The company had tried to do this by buying Ferrari but, when that plan failed, it decided to built its own racecar, using a new facility in Slough, England and with input from racecar specialist Lola.

The resulting car had a mid-mounted 4.2-litre Ford V8 engine which, in the early 1960s, was a radical solution when most other Le Mans racers were front-engined. Indeed, the design was based

▼ The GT40 from the rear, showing the mid-engine configuration

on the Lola GT which ran at Le Mans in 1963. The Ford was named GT40 because it stood just 40 inches high.

Three GT40s ran at Le Mans in 1964 and were fast but ultimately troublesome and they all retired from the event. However, Ford learned from the experience and returned the following year with an improved 'MkII' version that boasted a 7.0-litre Shelby engine. Again, though, the cars were unable to complete the demanding race. In 1966, however, Ford finally got it right and the modified MkII cars took Le Mans by storm, finishing in first, second and third places. The GT40's place in motoring history was guaranteed.

Ford continued to develop the GT40 for racing until 1968, by which time its competitors had moved on to such an extent that the GT40 was no longer competitive.

Around seven examples of a road-going GT40, the MkIII, were built between 1965 and 1969. This had a detuned 4.7-litre engine and radically restyled bodywork with four

SPECIFICATION (MK1)

Capacity: 4942cc

Cylinders: V8

Compression ratio: n/a

Maximum power: 425bhp at 6000rpm

Maximum torque: 540Nm at 4750rpm

Gearbox: Manual, five-speed

Length: 4343mm

Width: 1753mm

Weight: 950kg

0-60mph: 4.1 seconds

Maximum speed: 211mph

headlamps and a higher rear end to create some luggage space. However, it was not such an attractive-looking car, so most customers opted to have race versions converted for road use.

Only a very small number of genuine GT40s were built in total, but it has become one the great motoring legends and countless replicas have been produced over the years, ranging from cheap glassfibre kit cars, to very high quality hand-crafted aluminium replicas.

▲ The GT40 is low, at just 40 inches high

Ford GT

2003 USA

HOW TO SPOT

Retro-styled mid-engined coupe closely based on the 1960s' Ford GT40, but slightly larger and more angular. 'Ford GT' side decals and optional over-body stripes.

The Ford GT40 was a legendary Le Mans winner from the golden age of motorsport. So when Ford unveiled a concept car in 2002 that was a modern take on the classic, it caused enough of a frenzy for the company to put the car into limited production in 2003.

The new car was badged simply 'GT' because Ford did not have the rights to the 'GT40' name. Although it was styled after the classic racecar, the GT was very much a supercar for the road and, as such, was larger than the original.

Stunning performance – with a top speed of over 200mph and a 0-60mph time of just 3.3 seconds – came courtesy of a supercharged, all-aluminium, 5.4-litre V8 engine that produced 550bhp and generated a monumental 678Nm of torque. As before, the engine was

▼ The GT is very obviously styled after the classic GT40, but is larger all round

mid-mounted, but this time it drove the rear wheels through a modern six-speed gearbox. Under the gorgeous aluminium body lay a spaceframe chassis, also made from lightweight aluminium. Behind the 18-inch wheels were hugely powerful Brembo brakes with four-piston calipers.

Wealthy buyers in the 21st century demand much more than racing drivers in the 1960s, which was one reason the GT was larger than its inspiration. The more spacious interior was fully equipped with leather seats, climate control, electric windows, hi-fi, airbags, central locking and more. With its stylish perforated seats and alloy trim, the GT's cockpit was an inspiring place to be, even

▲ The GT's two-seater cockpit is modern but has been critisised for the quality of its fittings

if some of the trim looked a bit cheap. There was nothing particularly high-tech about the GT's execution. It was rear-wheel-drive with no traction control, other than ABS, and the suspension featured simple double-wishbones. Yet it worked surprisingly well, being very competent at high speed while, at the same time, remaining easy to drive. It was also relatively comfortable for a supercar, with acceptable ride quality for long-distance touring (although there was precious little luggage space).

The GT was a strictly limited-production car, with Ford building around 1500 a year over three years. That makes it less rare than a genuine GT40 but it nonetheless looks set to be a future classic, just like its predecessor.

SPECIFICATION

Capacity: 5409cc
Cylinders: V8
Compression ratio: 8.4:1
Maximum power: 550bhp at 6500rpm
Maximum torque: 678Nm at 3750rpm
Gearbox: Manual, six-speed
Length: 4643mm
Width: 1953mm
Weight: 1580kg
0-60mph: 3.3 seconds
Maximum speed: 205mph

Honda NSX

1990 Japan

HOW TO SPOT

Two-door coupe with low front with pop-up headlamps (up to 2002), rising to a high rear with integral spoiler. Angular side air intakes. Black-painted roof panel.

Supercars were, for many years, the preserve of the Europeans, with manufacturers such as Ferrari and Porsche dominating the market. On the other hand, Japanese car manufacturers were best known for producing reliable and well-engineered saloon cars.

So when Honda, which had an envious background with motorcycles and Formula 1 cars, unveiled its own supercar,

Europe sat up and took notice. And for good reason, too. The NSX had taken six years to develop, and it showed. Here was a car that combined high performance with comfort and usability.

Mounted transversely in the centre of the NSX was a 3.0-litre V6 engine that produced 270bhp. Made entirely of alloy and with four valves per cylinder, VTEC variable valve timing,

▼ The NSX has neat and understated lines, yet is nonetheless a true supercar

and titanium connecting rods, this could rev to 8300rpm – Honda's motorcycle influence, perhaps. Linked to the engine was a five-speed manual gearbox (or an optional automatic) driving the rear wheels.

The NSX's sleek and understated body may not have had the 'wow factor' of a European sports car, but it was nonetheless made from lightweight aluminium and – unusually for a car of this type – offered good all-round visibility.

And this ease of use extended throughout the NSX. You could get in it as easily as a saloon car, and the interior was practical and well laid-out,

SPECIFICATION

Capacity: 2977cc

Cylinders: V6

Compression ratio: 9.6:1

Maximum power: 270bhp at 7100rpm

Maximum torque: 284Nm at 5300rpm

Gearbox: Manual, five-speed

Length: 4425mm

Width: 1810mm

Weight: 1610g

0-60mph: 5.9 seconds

Maximum speed: 161mph

if a trifle ordinary. Passengers benefited from air-conditioning, decent stereo system, and remarkably civilised noise levels and ride quality. There was even a decent-sized luggage area behind the engine.

Even better, though, was that you got all this plus a car that was great fun to drive both in town and on the open road. At slow speeds, the NSX behaved impeccably, but get the revs up and it revealed another side to its character. The spirited engine propelled the car to 60mph in just 5.9 seconds and on to a top speed of 161mph, while the handling was hard to beat.

The NSX remained in production with minor changes until 2005. It may not have had the badge, but it was still a supercar; and one which you could happily use every day.

▲ The NSX's interior is businesslike and practical

Jaguar E-Type
1961 United Kingdom

▲ The E-Type with its oh-so-long bonnet is, for many, the ultimate sports car

The Jaguar E-Type is surely the quintessential British sports car of the 1960s. When it was unveiled in 1961 it took the world by storm. That long, long bonnet suggested speed and power, while the sleek, near-perfect looks were hard to beat in those days of boxy saloon cars.

The E-Type was available in hardtop form – with a novel (for the time) 'hatchback' rear window for luggage – and as an open-top roadster. Both versions were equally good-looking.

The huge one-piece bonnet tipped forward to give superb access to the engine. In the early cars was found a 3.8-litre straight-six, triple-carburettor engine from the XK150. This developed 265bhp and was capable of pushing the E-Type to speeds as high as 150mph. The six-cylinder engine was enlarged to 4.2-litre in 1966, then in 1971 a 5.3-litre V12 powerplant was installed.

By then, the E-Type had grown from a relatively light sports car into a two-plus-two grand-tourer. In order to fit two small seats in the back, the wheelbase was stretched and the roofline raised. While these later cars were undoubtedly roomier and more practical, they were not quite as elegant as the first E-Types.

The early cars had simple polished aluminium dashboards and small bucket seats. However, the equipment and comfort levels rose over the years, with better seats and more luxurious fittings.

The first E-Types had race-style cowls over the headlamps which looked

▲ Under the bonnet of this 1964 example is a 3.8-litre straight-six

wonderful but didn't conform to US regulations, so were deleted in 1968. The USA, incidentally, was the car's largest market, although emissions regulations stifled the power output. In North America the car was known as the Jaguar XK-E and around 80 percent of production went there.

The Jaguar E-Type remained in production until 1975 when it was replaced by the XJS, a car that failed to have the same long-term appeal as its predecessor. Yes, the E-Type is one of the world's great motoring legends; a car that defined a generation and has an everlasting appeal.

SPECIFICATION

Capacity: 3781cc

Cylinders: straight-six

Compression ratio: 9.0:1

Maximum power: 265bhp at 5500rpm

Maximum torque: 349Nm at 4000rpm

Gearbox: Four-speed manual

Length: 2438mm

Width: 1656mm

Weight: 1206kg

0-60mph: 7.0 seconds

Maximum speed: 150mph

Jaguar XJ220
1991 United Kingdom

HOW TO SPOT

Large, low and wide coupe with short bonnet and concealed headlamps. Long rear deck with integral spoiler. Scalloped sides with air intakes in rear wings.

When it was launched in 1991, the Jaguar XJ220 was the world's fastest car, with an incredible top speed of 213mph. A remarkable achievement when you consider that the car which made it into production was nothing like as sophisticated as the original concept.

The supercar which was unveiled to the public at the Birmingham motor show in 1988 was clearly inspired by the highly advanced Porsche 959. It was a huge but beautiful beast with a 6.2-litre V12 engine mounted amidships and

▼ A true big cat! The XJ220 is a large and powerful beast

powering all four wheels. The 200mph Jaguar also boasted forward-tilting doors and adaptive suspension – it promised to be a stunning machine.

A year later Ford took over Jaguar but, thankfully, agreed to progress the supercar project and build 350 production XJ220s. However, for economic reasons, the car's specification was much-reduced. Even though, it was said that each one would still cost a cool £361,000 – twice the price of a Ferrari F40!

The production car retained the

concept's sleek looks, but was slightly shorter and had conventional doors. The main changes, though, were hidden from sight. Gone was the 48-valve V12 engine and, in its place, came a 3.5-litre V6.

Still, buyers were not to be short-changed – the new engine boasted twin turbochargers and produced an impressive 542bhp, now driving the back wheels only. Also deleted was the trick suspension, in favour of conventional wishbones and coil springs.

A lot of time was spent developing the car's aerodynamics, to ensure a high top speed, but perhaps the main reason – after the engine – for the XJ220's impressive performance was its light weight; 1372kg was not a lot for a car of this size. The secret behind this was a bonded aluminium honeycomb body construction that was very light but at the same time strong.

Tests proved that the Jaguar could reach 213mph and its 0-60mph time was four seconds, while 100mph could be reached in just eight seconds. There was no doubt that the XJ220 was fast but it wasn't perfect. It was, quite simply, too big to be practical on most roads, and visibility was poor. It was also very expensive; by the time the car reached production in 1991 it cost no less than £403,000. In the end just 275 examples were built 1994.

Still, the Jaguar XJ220 is still one of the world's fastest cars, and one of Britain's few true supercars.

It's only a V6, but this compact engine was enough to make the XJ220 the world's fastest car

SPECIFICATION

Capacity: 3498cc
Cylinders: V6
Compression ratio: 8.3:1
Maximum power: 542bhp at 7200rpm
Maximum torque: 644Nm at4500rpm
Gearbox: Five-speed manual
Length: 4930mm
Width: 2007mm
Weight: 1372kg
0-60mph: 4.0 seconds
Maximum speed: 213mph

Jaguar XK

2005 United Kingdom

HOW TO SPOT

Muscular two-door coupe or roadster with wrap-around front and rear lights, oval Jaguar grille and integral rear spoiler.

The first Jaguar XK debuted IN 1996 to replace the XJS, and its svelte styling harked back to the glory days of the E-Type. It was an immediate success and helped Jaguar to regain its reputation as a manufacturer of high-quality, luxury performance cars.

In 2005 an all-new XK appeared which raises the ante in all respects. Like the contemporary XJ saloon, the new car had an all-aluminium bodyshell developed using aerospace technology to ensure it was immensely strong, rigid and – above all – light. Jaguar claimed that the new convertible XK was 48 percent more rigid and 140kg lighter than its predecessor. The design was very clearly a Jaguar, but more angular and aggressive-looking than the outgoing model.

Under the bonnet was a 4.2-litre V8 which was a development of that in the old XK. New fuel injection and variable valve timing helped ensure an output of 300bhp, while being more responsive and efficient than before.

The transmission was a six-speed automatic with manual shifts possible through fingertip controls on the steering wheel. The engine management system would even will blip the throttle for you during rapid downshifts.

More driver aids came in the form of active suspension that automatically adjusted to suit the road and the driving style, plus stability control that intervened when required to apply the brakes to individual wheels or reduce engine torque to help in critical handling situations.

As you'd expect of a Jaguar, the new

▼ The XK's interior is a pleasant mix of British luxury and modern features

XK's interior was plush and luxurious, with plenty of leather and wood on offer. A large screen in the centre console allowed you to control the climate control, satellite navigation, audio system and even linked with your Bluetooth mobile phone.

A neat feature was the optional Jaguar Smart Key System. Instead of a conventional ignition key, the XK had a keyfob that you keptp in your pocket or briefcase. When the car detected the proximity of this device, the engine could be started by means of the large red starter button. What's more, as you approached the Jaguar with the keyfob on your person, the car automatically unlocked itself for you. How cool is that?

The Jaguar XK offered a perfect blend of good looks, performance, luxury and practicality. It was a worthy successor to the original XK.

▲ The 2006 XK's styling draws on Jaguar's rich heritage without looking retro

SPECIFICATION

Capacity: 4196cc

Cylinders: V8

Compression ratio: n/a

Maximum power: 300bhp at 6000rpm

Maximum torque: 310Nm at 4100rpm

Gearbox: Six-speed sequential

Length: 4791mm

Width: 2070mm

Weight: 1595kg

0-60mph: 5.9 seconds

Maximum speed: 155mph

Jensen FF

1966 United Kingdom

HOW TO SPOT

Large coupe with long bonnet and roof-line. Twin slats in sides of front wings, curved glass rear hatch. Four headlamps in angular front grille.

The Jensen FF was billed as 'The World's most advanced car' for good reason. It was the four-wheel-drive version of the Jenson Interceptor and, as such, it was a revolutionary car. FF stood for 'Ferguson Four' after the tractor company that developed the transmission system. Driving all four wheels was, up until then, the preserve of off-road vehicles; this was the first time

▼ The stylish FF was the first sportscar with four-wheel-drive

that anyone had applied the principle to a sports car. And, indeed, it would be another 11 years before it would be done again; this time with the rather more successful Audi Quatro.

Four-wheel-drive was claimed to help get the power – and the FF had 325bhp – to the road without spinning the wheels, improve the handling, and make the car safer on slippery surfaces.

64

On the downside, though, the complex transmissions was heavy, expensive and sapped power.

As well as the novel transmission, the FF also boasted a Dunlop anti-lock braking system – many years before such devices became the norm. This car really was ahead of its time!

It was a large car, too, transporting two adults and two children in comfort and style. The interior was well-appointed with wood and leather, while the large opening tailgate allowed a useful amount of luggage to be carried. This really was a grand tourer.

Under that long and elegant bonnet lay a Chrysler V8 engine with a capacity of 6.2-litres. Linked to a three-speed automatic gearbox, it offered lazy power with plenty of torque. Despite the all-wheel transmission absorbing some of the power, it was still enough to waft the FF to 60mph in 8.5 seconds and on to a top speed of 130mph.

▲ The FF, with its massive rear window, held four people and luggage in comfort

The FF was sold alongside the Interceptor, which was essentially the same car but with conventional rear-wheel-drive and, therefore, better performance at a lower price. Whereas the FF was not a sales success and went out of production in 1971, the Interceptor was sold until 1976. It then went back into production in very limited numbers between 1983 and 1992.

Only 224 examples of the Jensen FF were ever built and it's often forgotten about when people talk about the history of four-wheel-drive sports cars. The FF does, however, mark the start of an exciting new era; even if it was many years ahead of its time.

SPECIFICATION

Capacity: 6276cc
Cylinders: V8
Compression ratio: 10.0:1
Maximum power: 325bhp at 4600rpm
Maximum torque: 576Nm at 2800rpm
Gearbox: Three-speed automatic
Length: 4572mm
Width: 1778mm
Weight: 1564kg
0-60mph: 8.5 seconds
Maximum speed: 130mph

Lamborghini Miura

1966 Italy

Italian Ferruccio Lamborghini made his fortune building tractors and enjoyed driving fast cars; namely Ferraris. However, he was disappointed by the build quality of these cars and, when he complained, Enzo Ferrari told Lamborghini to stick to building tractors and leave him to worry about cars. That's the legend anyway.

Whatever the truth, the fact is that

▼The Miura was World-breaking with its mid-engined layout, which led to its stunning looks

Lamborghini decided to build his own supercar and the result was the 350 GTV of 1963. That front-engined car was good, but not remarkable. It's replacement, the Miura, was both these things and much more.

The Miura of 1966 shocked the supercar world and changed it forever. Why? Because its engine was not mounted at the front, but in the middle. This gave

Very low mid-engine coupe with pop-up headlamps with 'lashes'. Air intakes in centre of bonnet, and further ones behind each side window. Louvres above engine.

near-perfect weight distribution which, in turn, helped give superb handling. It's a configuration that most supercars – and some lesser sports cars – use to this day.

Unusually, though, the 4.0-litre V12 was mounted transversely, which meant it could fit behind the seats and in front of the rear axle without the car being overly long. It's an idea that debuted in – of all things – the Mini, which had a transverse engine at the front.

The mid-engined layout meant that the Bertone-designed body could be low and sleek. The nose, in particular, is very low and is distinguished by pop-up headlamps with, on early examples, were framed by air intakes for the front brakes that looked a bit like eyelashes. At the rear, meanwhile, a set of louvres helped engine cooling and gave some rear visibility.

The Miura was gradually developed over the years, with improvements to the chassis and engine. The SV version of 1971 boasted 385bhp, a wider track, improved suspension and a stiffer bodyshell. A one-off open-top Miura was produced for the 1968 Brussels motor show, but this never went into production.

The Miura was not perfect   it had a tendency for the front-end to lift at high speed – but it set the tone for supercars to follow; not least its own successor, the Lamborghini Countach of 1974. It does, though, remain one of the most beautiful cars of all time.

▲ A distinctive feature of the Miura were its headlamps with vents top and bottom that looked like eyelashes

SPECIFICATION

Capacity: 3929cc
Cylinders: V12
Compression ratio: 9.8:1
Maximum power: 350bhp at 7000rpm
Maximum torque: 369Nm at 3850rpm
Gearbox: Five-speed manual
Length: 4255mm
Width: 1803mm
Weight: 1292kg
0-60mph: 6.0 seconds
Maximum speed: 171mph

Lotus Esprit V8

1996 United Kingdom

HOW TO SPOT

Low, wide, wedge-shaped coupe with cabin thrust forward and long rear deck behind. Pop-up headlamps and large rear wing.

The Lotus Esprit dates right back to 1975. The original car was extremely angular and powered by a mid-mounted four-cylinder engine that developed 156bhp, or 210bhp in turbocharged form. Over the years, the square lines were rounded off as fashion changed, and the twin-cam engine was refined with more power.

However, the Esprit's biggest leap forward came in 1996 when, for the top models, the four-pot engine was thrown out in favour of an all-new V8. This 3.5-litre unit was cleverly designed by Lotus to be compact, light and – above all – powerful. Twin Garrett turbochargers assured an output of 349bhp which put the Esprit, at last, into true supercar league, with a 0-60mph time of 4.7 seconds and a top speed of 175mph. The power was controlled by a manual five-

▼The Esprit V8 retained the original car's wedge shape, but with softer lines

speed gearbox driving the rear wheels.

Yet there was more to the Esprit than sheer performance. Right from the start, the mid-engined, glassfibre, car was renowned for its handling; Lotus's chassis engineers did a superb job of creating a perfectly balanced sports car that was a joy to drive.

SPECIFICATION

Capacity: 3506cc
Cylinders: V8
Compression ratio: 8.0:1
Maximum power: 349bhp at 6500rpm
Maximum torque: 400Nm at 4250rpm
Gearbox: Five-speed manual
Length: 4369mm
Width: 1883mm
Weight: 1380kg
0-60mph: 4.7 seconds
Maximum speed: 175mph

In 1998, the Esprit V8 was treated to a smart new interior that eliminated the old car's rather dated dash layout. Strictly a two-seater, you sat low with a wide centre console between you and your passenger. However, the interior didn't have the air of quality expected of a supercar at the end of the 20th century.

An extreme lightweight V8 appeared in 1999 and was badged Sport 350. A limited edition of just 50 cars, each was finished in silver with a blue interior and massive rear wing. By reducing the weight by 80kg and remapping the engine to give more torque at low revs (the overall power remained unchanged), Lotus created the fastest and most exciting Esprit ever.

Sadly, though, the model was really showing its age by now, and the Esprit finally went out of production in 2004, after 29 years. Flawed it may have been, but it was still a great British supercar and a fantastic-looking one at that.

▲ Despite dating back to the 1970s, the Esprit's shape still looks stunning today

Lotus Exige Cup 240
2006 United Kingdom

The Lotus Elise of 1995 marked a return to basics for Lotus; the tiny roadster was the spiritual successor of the Lotus Seven (now the Caterham Seven). It was fun, fast and affordable.

In 2000, Lotus produced a Sport Elise for racing, which had 200bhp and a fixed roof. Such was the interest in this pocket racer that Lotus went on to build a production version.

This was the Exige.

The original Exige had a mid-mounted four-cylinder K-series engine that produced 190bhp – a lot of power in a car that weighed less than 1000kg. The low weight was thanks to a high-tech epoxy-bonded aluminium chassis and glassfibre body panels. The Exige was a pure driving machine, with lively performance and superb handling, all unhindered by

▼ The tiny Exige Cup in its home environment – a racetrack

Tiny mid-engined two-seater with slanted headlamps, two large intakes in top of bonnet, air scoop in roof and large rear wing.

weight or complex electronics found on most other modern sports cars.

Adding a fixed roof in place of the Elise's soft-top allowed Lotus to place a distinctive air scoop on the top of the car, which fed air into the engine. Black grilles over the engine aided cooling, but didn't do anything for rear visibility.

As great as the original Exige was, it couldn't be sold in the all-important US market because the K-series engine didn't comply with local emissions regulations, so in 2004, Lotus announced the Exige S2 with a Toyota engine, which offered similar performance.

SPECIFICATION

Capacity: 1796cc
Cylinders: Straight-four
Compression ratio: 10.9:1
Maximum power: 243bhp at 8000rpm
Maximum torque: 236Nm at 8000rpm
Gearbox: Six-speed manual
Length: 3797mm
Width: 1850mm
Weight: 875kg
0-60mph: 4.5 seconds
Maximum speed: 150mph

This new engine had the potential for further tuning, though, which made possible the Exige Cup 240. This had essentially the same engine but enhanced with a Rootes supercharger that boosts power to 243bhp. In the same lightweight body, this gave astonishing performance, with 60mph being reached in 5 seconds and a top speed of 150mph – not bad for a 1.8-litre engine! The engine was linked to a six-speed gearbox and limited-slip differential driving the rear wheels.

Designed as a track car that can also be used on the road, the Cup 240 came complete with roll-cage, harnesses, fire extinguisher system and ignition kill-switch. What you didn't get, of course, were any luxuries – not even a radio.

At almost £50,000, the Exige Cup 240 was not a cheap car, but it did give a mouth-watering blend of power and lightness which was hard to beat at any price.

▲ The Cup's interior is very much that of a racecar, with full rollcage and fire extinguishing system

Marcos TSO-GT2

2005 United Kingdom

HOW TO SPOT

Aggressive two-seater coupe with sweeping lines. Long bonnet with cowled headlamps, fins along front wings, and fastback rear window.

The TSO-GT2 followed a long tradition of Marcos sports cars. The company was founded in Luton in 1959 by Frank Costin and Jem Marsh. Their first vehicles were kit cars that, unusually, used plywood in their construction. The company went through mixed fortunes and produced a range of different models over the years, before turning its back on kit cars in 1992 to concentrate on the fully-built Mantura sports car, which was powered by a Rover V8 engine.

After going out of business (not for the first time) in 2000, the company was bought by an American investor

▼ The TSO is a surprisingly small car, but a very capable one, nonetheless

and a new range of cars was launched, including the exciting TSO-GT2 in 2005.

The surprisingly small TSO-GT2 had obvious Marcos styling cues, including headlamps under plastic cowls and a distinctive rear end that harked back to Marcos designs from the 1960s. It was, however, a very modern car under the skin. The high-quality glassfibre bodyshell was attached to a light but stiff tubular steel spaceframe chassis.

Under that long bonnet lay a 5.7-litre Chevrolet V8 that was tuned to produce a hefty 475bhp together with 535Nm of torque. Driving the rear wheels, this gave explosive performance with a top speed of 185mph and a 0-60mph time

▲ The TSO's interior is small but well-appointed

of just 4 seconds. To help keep this power in check, the car's suspension was developed in conjunction with rally experts Prodrive.

Inside the TSO-GT2 was a compact but very distinctive two-seater cockpit. A concave aluminium dashboard housed a cluster of centrally-mounted instruments with retro-style cream faces. The rest of the interior was hand-trimmed in high-quality leather, while the steering wheel was surprisingly upright. It was undoubtedly a unique place to be.

The Marcos TSO-GT2 may not have been the most sophisticated sports car ever built, but it was exciting and full of character at a time when mass-produced cars were becoming more and more similar and soulless.

SPECIFICATION

Capacity: 5665cc
Cylinders: V8
Compression ratio: 10.1:1
Maximum power: 475bhp at 6500rpm
Maximum torque: 535Nm at 5500rpm
Gearbox: Manual, six-speed
Length: 4020mm
Width: 1680mm
Weight: 1170kg
0-60mph: 4.0 seconds
Maximum speed: 185mph

Maserati Bora

1971 Italy

HOW TO SPOT

Mid-engined coupe with unpainted stainless-steel roof and windscreen pillars. Side windows curve upwards into high rear-end with near-horizontal rear window and long, narrow rear quarter windows.

In the late 1960S and early 1970S, the Italian Maserati company was owned by Citroën and it was during this time that the stunning-looking Bora – the first mid-engined production Maserati – was conceived. Here was a car that was undoubtedly a high-power supercar but, at the same time, looked modest and understated.

▼ The Bora was an elegant and understated supercar. Note the stainless-steel roof

Perhaps the most extraordinary thing about the Giugiaro design was its roof and windscreen pillars. Those were made from unpainted satin-finish stainless-steel which, from a distance, made it look as if the car had a glass roof. Behind that was an almost horizontal glass panel which lifted to gain access to the engine bay.

The Bora's cockpit was comfortable and well-equipped for its time

The engine was a 4.7-litre V8 driving the rear wheels. With 310bhp on tap, it gave very respectable levels of performance for the time, with a top speed in excess of 160mph. To rein in this power, the Bora had a very unusual braking system, thanks to its Citroën parentage. Instead of a conventional arrangement, the car had a high-pressure hydraulic system, driven from the engine. Similar hydraulics were used for powering the lift-up headlamps, the adjustable driver's seat, pedals and even the steering column.

The reason for the adjustable pedals was because the driver's seat didn't actually move fore and aft – the pedals moved instead, to adjust for different heights of driver. It is claimed that when cars were ordered new, the seats were adapted to suit the owner's build.

In 1976, fuel prices escalated and Citroën parted company with Maserati. The Bora remained in production, latterly with a 4.9-litre engine, until 1978; by which time 571 examples had been built. Meanwhile, though, Maserati was also selling its 'baby Bora'; the more popular Merak, which had the same body but was powered by a more economical 2.0-litre V6 engine, and didn't have the complex Citroën hydraulic systems. Around 1500 Meraks were built by the time production ceased in 1983.

The Bora remains one of the most elegant Maseratis of all time, and the unusual technology it embraces continues to fascinate enthusiasts.

SPECIFICATION

Capacity: 4719cc
Cylinders: V8
Compression ratio: 8.5:1
Maximum power: 310bhp at 7500rpm
Maximum torque: 440Nm at 4200rpm
Gearbox: Manual, five-speed
Length: 4335mm
Width: 1768mm
Weight: 1520g
0-60mph: 6.5 seconds
Maximum speed: 162mph

Maserati MC12

2004 Italy

HOW TO SPOT

Very long race-style coupe with 'bubble' cockpit, air intake on roof, sweeping wings, finned intakes in top of bonnet and large rear spoiler.

After a 37-year break in motorsport, Maserati wanted to enter a car into the GT category of the Le Mans 24-hour race, and to do so the company had to produce a minimum of 25 road-going examples of the car for customers.

That car was the MC12 – essentially a road-going Le Mans racer and, as such, it wa very long and low, with classic Le Mans lines. Developed in a wind-tunnel, the body was made from lightweight but strong carbonfibre honeycomb and it had a removable roof panel for open-air motoring.

Power came courtesy of a mid-mounted, Ferrari-developed V12 engine that produced 623bhp – very useful in a car that weighed just 1335kg. Indeed, it was enough to propel the MC12 to 60mph in 3.8

▼It looks more like a Le Mans racer, but the MC12 is actually road-legal

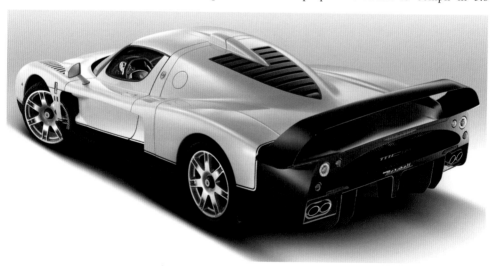

seconds and onto a top speed of 205mph. The rear-mounted gearbox was controlled by fingertip paddles on the steering column, as has become the norm for racing cars, and the power went straight to the back wheels.

Despite its racing heritage, the MC12 was a surprisingly civilised car to travel in, with tolerable levels of noise and comfort. The cockpit was well appointed with leather and carbonfibre, and benefited from climate control and there was even the trademark oval Maserati clock on the centre console. It was everything you'd expect of a grand tourer.

SPECIFICATION

Capacity: 5998cc
Cylinders: V12
Compression ratio: 11.2:1
Maximum power: 623bhp at 7500rpm
Maximum torque: 652Nm at 5500rpm
Gearbox: Manual, six-speed
Length: 5143mm
Width: 2096mm
Weight: 1335kg
0-60mph: 3.8 seconds
Maximum speed: 205mph

The only problem, though, was that the MC12 was enormous – no less than two feet longer than a Ferrari Enzo, and a foot wider. Which meant that it wasn't an easy machine to manoeuvre; especially when you consider that there was no rear window whatsoever! But then supercars are not meant to be practical, are they? This, however, was surely one of the most impractical ever built!

Never mind, get on the open road and put your foot down to get the full effect of those 623 horses and any worries about practicality soon vanished as you experienced the sheer performance of this Italian supercar. And with only 25 examples worldwide, you could be assured of exclusivity wherever you went.

▲ The MC12's cockpit is surprisingly luxurious. It even has the trademark Maserati clock!

Maserati GranSport

2005 Italy

▲ The GranSport is elegant and understated

Maserati and Ferrari used to be competitors but are now part of the same Fiat organisation. To avoid the two marques clashing, therefore, Ferrari is the hardcore sports brand, while Maseratis are more luxurious grand tourers. This was demonstrated perfectly by the GranSport, a powerful machine that could transport two adults and two children in extreme comfort and speed over long distances. It was a development of the 3200GT – which dates back to 1998 – and the more recent Coupe, but was substantially updated and improved.

Under that elegant bonnet lay a V8 engine that produced 400bhp and could propel the Maserati at speeds of up to 180mph. It was linked to a six-speed transmission with fingertip changers; this was a car that was designed for the

Large two-plus-two coupe with low waist-line and distinctive grille with Maserati 'trident' badge. Downward curve to each side of boot.

enthusiastic family driver. Maserati called its gearshift system Cambiocorsa, and it was electronically controlled with a choice of four settings – Normal, Sport, Automatic and Low Grip.

The handling, too, would please the sporty pilot, but excellent road-holding does not come at the expense of comfort; unlike some extreme coupes, this one did not offer a rock-hard ride. Yes, it was firm, but remained compliant enough to be comfortable on all but the bumpiest roads. An option was Skyhook adaptive damping which automatically adjusted to suit the driving style and road conditions.

Inside, you found even more comfort, but was not just the traditional leather that you might expect. Yes, there was plenty of high-quality hide on the seats and dash, but you also found something quite unusual. It was a 'technical' fabric developed for the nautical industry and almost resembled carbonfibre but was flexible, non-slip and extremely hard-wearing, making it ideal for trimming the central area of the seats, the lower rim of the steering wheel and the central part of the dash. It looked refreshingly different.

A Maserati of any sort is a quirky purchase and you'd think twice about choosing one over, say, a Porsche 911 for similar money. But it is a car with class and luxury, and is just that little bit different to the norm.

▲Unlike most supercars, the GranSport has room in the back for two passengers

SPECIFICATION

Capacity: 4244cc
Cylinders: V8
Compression ratio: 11.2:1
Maximum power: 400bhp at 7500rpm
Maximum torque: 451Nm at 4500rpm
Gearbox: Manual, six-speed
Length: 4523mm
Width: 1822mm
Weight: 1580kg
0-60mph: 4.8 seconds
Maximum speed: 180mph

McLaren F1
1993 United Kingdom

HOW TO SPOT

Compact and low coupe with cabin thrust forward. Scalloped sides with distinctive strakes. Roof-mounted air-scoop and forward-pivoting doors.

▼ The F1's neat and taut lines were designed for aerodynamic efficiency above all else

When Gordon Murray, of Formula 1 manufacturer McLaren, decided to build a supercar, the world knew it would be something special. As it turned out, the McLaren F1 was more than just special – it was out of this world.

Unlike some other supercars, the F1 was relatively small, making it easier to drive on public roads. Styled by Peter Stevens, it looked purposeful but restrained – as you'd expect of a true British car – the only concession to outrageousness being a pair of forward-opening doors.

But there was nothing restrained underneath that rear engine cover. The mid-mounted 627bhp powerplant was a purpose-built BMW V12 with a 6-litre capacity. In a nod to McLaren's racing heritage, drive was to the rear wheels only, via a manual six-speed gearbox.

The bodywork was extremely light in weight because it borrowed from Formula 1 technology. It consisted of a carbonfibre monocoque reinforced by aluminium honeycomb panels, which combined to give a very light but strong structure. With a weight of just 1137kg, the powerful engine propelled the car to 60mph in just 3.2 seconds, 100mph in a mere 6.5 seconds, and on to a blistering top speed of 240mph. No other road car had ever come near such figures, and the McLaren was by far the fastest car in

the world – a title it held onto until the launch of the even wilder Bugatti Veyron in 2005.

Inside, the F1 had a novel arrangement; the driver sat in the centre of the car, surrounded by a passenger seat on each side. The driver's seat was forward of the passengers', to ensure good visibility. This set-up made it awkward to get in and out, but once in place, you had a near-perfect driving position, and it was suitable for driving on the left or the right. The F1 also had the advantage of being able to seat three people, whereas most supercars were strictly two-seaters.

The F1 had a price tag as astonishing

▲ Massive Brembo brakes help tame the F1's power

SPECIFICATION

Capacity: 6064cc
Cylinders: V12
Compression ratio: 10.5:1
Maximum power: 627bhp at 7400rpm
Maximum torque: 1250Nm at 2200-5500rpm
Gearbox: Manual, six-speed
Length: 4290mm
Width: 1820mm
Weight: 1137kg
0-60mph: 3.2 seconds
Maximum speed: 240mph

as its performance – over half a million Pounds – and only 100 examples were built by the time production ended at the end of 1997.

The McLaren remains one of the world's ultimate supercars. Its sensible size, modest appearance, light weight, high performance, phenomenal handling and exquisite build quality remain unbeaten to this day. Indeed, it's unlikely there will ever be another car like it.

Mercedes-Benz SLR McLaren

2005 Germany/United Kingdom

In 1995, Mercedes-Benz and McLaren joined forces to create a formidable Formula 1 team. And just four years later, the partnership revealed the SLR Vision concept car. This stunning road-going machine finally went into production, with just some changes (and minus the 'Vision' name), in 2005.

The SLR's styling drew inspiration from the classic Mercedes SL coupe of the 1950s, as well as the recent McLaren-Mercedes Formula 1 cars. The forward-pivoting doors hinted at the SL's gullwing doors, while the pointed nose was a shameless nod to Formula 1 design. The long bonnet and the cabin pushed right back gave the range-topping Mercedes a traditionally aggressive and powerful appearance, which was refreshingly different to that of most mid-engined supercars.

The SLR monocoque was of strong but light carbonfibre, just like a Formula 1 car, and was built by McLaren in the UK. This material was about half the weight of steel for the same strength.

▼ The SLR is an imposing car with its long bonnet and distinctive lines

Two-door coupe with very long bonnet with bulge narrowing towards nose. Forward-hinging doors and distinctive vents and strakes in front wings.

Under the long bonnet was an AMG-built V8 engine set well back in the car to give an almost 50:50 weight distribution front to rear – called a 'front mid-engine' configuration. The all-alloy power unit was supercharged and develops 626bhp, together with a hefty 780Nm of torque from as low as 3250rpm. In such a lightweight body, this was enough to give the SLR true supercar performance – the top speed was 207mph, and 0-60mph took a mere 3.8 seconds.

Yet the SLR was very different to most supercars. Being front-engined meant that it was much more practical than a mid-engined car. You got good all-round visibility, for starters; while the boot was large enough for two sets of golf clubs or enough luggage for two people to take a touring holiday.

The SLR was more of a super grand tourer than a racecar for the road. Inside, passengers were cosseted in high-quality leather seats and there were all the luxuries you'd expect of a top-class sports saloon. A neat feature was the engine-start button hidden under a flip-up lid on the gear selector knob. The transmission,

incidentally, was automatic.

The Mercedes-Benz SLR McLaren was an eye-catching car with its Batmobile-like styling, and performance to match. You wouldn't expect anything less from the pairing of two great companies.

▲ This cutout shows how far back the SLR's engine sits. You can also see the unusual doors

SPECIFICATION

Capacity: 5496cc
Cylinders: V8
Compression ratio: 8.8:1
Maximum power: 626bhp at 6500rpm
Maximum torque: 780Nm at 3250rpm
Gearbox: Five-speed automatic
Length: 4655mm
Width: 1907mm
Weight: 1692kg
0-60mph: 3.8 seconds
Maximum speed: 207mph

MG Metro 6R4

1984 United Kingdom

HOW TO SPOT

Metro body shape with massive, boxy front and rear wheel-arch extensions, deep sill extensions with large side air intakes above. Massive front and rear spoilers.

Some cars are so silly you just have to love them. And the MG Metro 6R4 is right up there with the best. Surely only a British company could have the audacity to turn a mundane town car into an outrageous rally beast.

In the early 1980s, Group B rally cars were able to have very high levels of power, and in order to compete on the world stage, Austin-Rover had to come up with something very special.

The standard Austin Metro was as dull as they came, but there was very little of the standard car in the 6R4 (the name, incidentally, means six-cylinders; rear engine; four-wheel-drive). Out went the front-mounted A-series engine and in came a purpose-built V6 unit mounted amidships, where you'd normally find the back seats.

The 3-litre, all-alloy engine was developed with the help of Cosworth and had twin camshafts per cylinder head and four valves per cylinder. Unlike many of its competitors, it was not turbocharged, but even so it could be tuned to produce as much as 410bhp, although most pumped out between 250bhp and 380bhp. The power was fed to all four wheels via a five-speed gearbox and Ferguson-developed transmission system.

As impressive as the drivetrain was, it was the bodywork that really caught people's attention. Here was a car that was certainly not designed for its looks. The basic shape of the Metro remained – albeit largely formed from plastic – but was mostly hidden under huge plastic

▼ A 6R4 doing what it does best at the 1985 RAC rally

wheel arch and sill extensions, needed to accommodate the wider track. Big front and rear spoilers helped to push the car onto the road at high speed.

Inside, the rear was completely given over to the engine, while the front seats were supportive race items with four-point harnesses. As you'd expect, there was no carpeting although, bizarrely, the standard Metro dash and door panels remained, while the steering wheel was

▲ Coping with the mud at the 1986 RAC Rally

from the Maestro.

It may have looked ridiculous, but the 6R4's performance was nothing to laugh about. Figures depended on engine specification and gearing, but the car could rocket to 60mph in as little as 4.3-seconds. Top speed could be as much as 155mph.

Sadly, the 6R4 never got a chance to prove itself on the rally circuit because, after a series of high-profile crashes, Group B competition was banned, and the age of wild rally cars came to an end. However, 6R4s have continued to compete in other events over the years and the engine went on to form the basis of the Jaguar XJ220, after the rights were bought by Tom Walkinshaws Racing.

SPECIFICATION

Capacity: 2991cc

Cylinders: V6

Compression ratio: 12.0:1

Maximum power: 410bhp at 6500rpm

Maximum torque: 362Nm at 6500rpm

Gearbox: Manual, five-speed

Length: 3350mm

Width: 1880mm

Weight: 1040kg

0-60mph: 4.3 seconds

Maximum speed: 155mph

MG X-Power SV-R

2004 United Kingdom

HOW TO SPOT

Long, louvred bonnet, and further large louvres in each front wing. Large wheel-arch extensions, deep front spoiler and optional rear wing

It was an odd thing for a struggling UK car company to do; buy a struggling Italian sports car design that was sold in the US and revamp it as a high-power supercar that wouldn't be sold in the USA.

Yet that is just what MG Rover did. The MG X-Power SV was based on the Qvale Mangusta, but heavily restyled and re-engineered as a pure sports car.

▼The SV-R is an MG like no other – wild to look at and wild to drive

It was an imposing car, the SV; long, low and wide, with air intakes and spoilers everywhere you looked. Pretty, it was not, but it certainly looked as if it meant business. The bodyshell was made of lightweight carbonfibre and enveloped a steel box-frame chassis. The shape was honed in a wind tunnel, while the traditional long bonnet gave away the fact that the engine was mounted at the front.

Actually, to be precise, the SV was 'front mid-engined'. In other words, the engine was set right back in the chassis to give a well-balanced weight distribution.

Two versions were produced; the standard 320bhp SV and the more powerful SV-R you see here, which developed a heady 385bhp.

The relatively simple American V8 engine had a capacity of 5-litres and relied on sheer size to develop its power, instead of bolt-on turbo- or superchargers. And with 510Nm of torque on-tap, it was a lazy, easy-to-live-with sort of power.

But floor the throttle, and all that power going through just the rear

wheels was a far from lazy experience. Surprisingly, though, the SV-R was a well-balanced and light car to drive, with superb handling characteristics.

The two-seater interior was fully finished in leather and Alcantara, with aluminium trim hinting at MG's heritage. Each car was hand-built to order, so customers could choose their own interior and exterior colours and finishes.

Sadly, as good as the SV-R was, it was not a sales success – at over £80,000 it was a lot of money for an MG – and it could be argued that the company made a mistake investing in such a niche-market product.

MG Rover went out of business in 2005, after producing only a handful of SVs. Those few cars that were built are testimony to an enthusiastic group of designers and engineers who let their hearts lead their heads to develop an exciting British supercar. And in that they certainly succeeded!

▲ The rear of the SV-R with the optional rear spoiler

SPECIFICATION

Capacity: 4996cc

Cylinders: V8

Compression ratio: 11.4:1

Maximum power: 385bhp at 6000rpm

Maximum torque: 510Nm at 4750rpm

Gearbox: Manual, five-speed

Length: 4480mm

Width: 2670mm

Weight: 1500kg

0-60mph: 4.9 seconds

Maximum speed: 175mph

MINI Cooper S Works

2003 United Kingdom

▲ A MINI on steriods! Note the neat 'Works' badge on the lower grille

The Cooper name has been inextricably linked with MINI since the original MINI Cooper was launched in 1961. In those early days, John Cooper uprated standard MINIs to make them even more fun to drive, and had some success racing his modified MINIs in the 1960s.

Before long, BMC realised the appeal of the Cooper name and began producing its own 'official' MINI Coopers, paying royalties for the use of the name. John Cooper, however, continued to develop his own tuning kits and, after the production MINI Cooper was discontinued in 1971, he kept producing his own upgrades for loyal enthusiasts.

When the new MINI was launched in 2001, parent company BMW again produced a sporting version with the revered Cooper badge on the back. A more

Distinctive MINI body shape enhanced with large bonnet air intake, side intakes in front wings, alloy fuel-filler cap, centrally-mounted twin exhaust tailpipe, 'Works' badging.

powerful incarnation, the Cooper S, boasted a supercharged engine.

Sadly, John Cooper died before he could see this exciting new generation of MINIs, but his son Mike kept the company going, under the name John Cooper Works, and soon developed his own upgrades for the factory Cooper and Cooper S.

The Works tuning kit for the Cooper S produced a heady 210bhp, which was a worthwhile 40bhp more than standard. The extra power came courtesy of an uprated supercharger, tuned cylinder head, sports air intake and exhaust, and the ubiquitous engine-management upgrades.

In addition, John Cooper Works offered uprated brakes and suspension, 18-inch alloy wheels, and sports seats, not to mention tasteful body and interior upgrades.

The extra power transformed an already superb car. With 60mph coming up in just 6.6 seconds and a top speed of 143mph, the Cooper S Works was a seriously fast MINI and not a car to be taken lightly.

In 2005, BMW began to offer the Works kit as a factory option on brand-new MINIs and as a retrofit upgrade through its dealers, thus endorsing it as a fully approved performance package.

Any new MINI is great fun, the Cooper S especially so. Add the Works magic into the equation and you had one very special car, indeed. With sparkling performance, leach-like handling, cheeky looks and a well-appointed, comfortable interior; all at a sensible price. What more could you want? The MINI Cooper S Works really was an affordable supercar.

The MINIs interior is very well equipped. This one even has sat-nav

SPECIFICATION

Capacity: 1598cc
Cylinders: straight four
Compression ratio: 8.3:1
Maximum power: 210bhp at 6950rpm
Maximum torque: 245Nm at 4500rpm
Gearbox: Manual, six-speed. Optional Steptronic
Length: 3655mm
Width: 1688mm
Weight: 1140kg
0-60mph: 6.6 seconds
Maximum speed: 143mph

Mitsubishi Lancer Evolution IX

2006 Japan

The 'Evo' as was commonly known, first appeared in 1992. It was initially an homologation special to enable Mitsubishi to enter the World Rally Championship's Group A class and the SCCA Pro Rally Championship. Based on the Lancer saloon car, the first Evos were only officially sold in Japan but some entered Europe as grey-market imports, until official imports to the UK started in 1998.

The first Evolution had a 2.0-litre engine that produced 244bhp and drove all four wheels through a five-speed gearbox. It was to set the trend for all future Evos – and there have been plenty! Over the years, the model was developed in tandem with the standard Lancer saloon and the power and handling improved as time went on;

▼ The Evo may not be much to look at, but it knows how to perform!

Mid-sized four-door saloon with angular nose, offset front numberplate and bonnet scoop. Massive rear spoiler.

although the car's weight also increased. The name Evolution turned out to be very apt – this was a car that gradually evolved over time.

The Evolution IX of 2006 was the last of the line before an all-new model replaced it. By this time, the Evo boasted a six-speed gearbox, Super Active Yaw Control, an aluminium roof to save weight and a larger carbonfibre rear wing. The engine remained a 2.0-litre turbocharged unit but by now it produced 345bhp and 435Nm of torque, thanks to a number of improvements including – for the first time – variable valve control. In standard form this was enough to record the car to 60mph in 4.3 seconds and on to a top speed of 157mph.

However, the Evo was known for more than just its power: it was one of the best-handling saloon cars ever. This was thanks to its four-wheel-drive low centre of gravity, Bilstein dampers and yaw control There wasn't much that could beat an Evo from A to B on winding roads or track.

In 2005 Mitsubishi unveiled the Concept-X show car that hinted what the next-generation Evolution X may be like. While still obviously an Evo, it had a sleeker more modern body and was, once again, very much an evolution of the previous cars.

▲ The Evo's interior is typical of a Japanese saloon car

Capacity: 1997cc
Cylinders: Straight four
Compression ratio: 8.8:1
Maximum power: 345bhp at 6800rpm
Maximum torque: 435Nm at 4600rpm
Gearbox: Manual, six-speed
Length: 4490mm
Width: 1770mm
Weight: 1400kg
0-60mph: 4.3 seconds
Maximum speed: 157mph

Morgan Aero Eight

2000 United Kingdom

Morgan is a traditional British car manufacturer, based in the Malvern Hills. It's been producing its 4/4 model since 1936, so it was quite a shock when the company announced a brand-new model in 2000. And it was even more of a shock when the new car was unveiled!

The Aero 8 looked like no other Morgan; or, indeed, like any other car. Designed with the aid of a wind tunnel, it had essentially the traditional Morgan shape, but smoothed and updated to ensure a better drag co-efficient. Perhaps the strangest thing about the Aero 8's appearance were its headlamps, which were swept back but also appeared to point inwards, giving the car a cross-eyed look.

Morgans have traditionally been built

▼ The Aero 8 is an odd but strangely elegant car

92

on an ash frame, and the Aero 8 was no exception. However, the aluminium bodywork rode on a high-tech bonded aluminium chassis and the ash-work visible inside the cockpit was more for show.

The suspension, too, was a leap away from traditional Morgan technology, which relied on an antiquated sliding pillar system. The Aero 8 had, instead, a fully independent double wishbone set-up with race-quality joints. This, at last, was a Morgan that handled well.

And it needed to handle well, too, with 325bhp on tap. The power came, not from a Rover V8 like previous Morgans, but from a modern BMW 4.4-litre engine

▲ The Aero 8's cockpit is an attractive mix of retro and modern. Note the exposed ashwork

from the 5-scrics. This was linked to a modern six-speed Getrag gearbox driving the rear wheels. In a relatively lightweight car, the engine ensured good performance, with 60mph coming up in 4.7 seconds and on a top speed of 160mph.

Inside, occupants enjoyed a mix of traditional and modern. There was plenty of wood, aluminium and leather on show, of course, but you also benefited from electrically heated windows all round, a CD player, plus optional air-conditioning and satellite navigation. The luggage area, meanwhile, had room for a set of golf clubs.

The Morgan Aero 8 was a car people either loved or hated. But if you ignored its bizarre appearance, you had a truly great and unique motorcar.

SPECIFICATION

Capacity: 4398cc

Cylinders: V8

Compression ratio: 10.0:1

Maximum power: 325bhp at 6100rpm

Maximum torque: 330Nm at 360rpm

Gearbox: Six-speed manual

Length: 4120mm

Width: 1770mm

Weight: 1132kg

0-60mph: 4.7 seconds

Maximum speed: 160mph

Nissan 350Z

2003 Japan

HOW TO SPOT

Taut two-door coupe with small, curving side windows. Distinctively shaped front and rear lights with narrow vertical indicators on front quarters. Large rectangular front intake.

In 1969 Nissan – or Datsun as IT was then known – introduced a fantastic sports coupe. Called the 240Z, it combined muscle-car looks and lively performance with Japanese affordability and reliability. It was the poor man's E-Type but, at the same time, a great car in its own right. Sadly, though, it didn't last. Sure, the Z range continued over the years with the 260Z, 280Z and 300Z, but these were bloated compared with the original and, in 1996, the Z range was dropped.

And then, in 2003, Nissan brought out the brand-new 350Z which returned to the original concept of the 240Z. The car's squat and compact looks were inspired by the 240Z (and, if we're honest, by Audi's TT) but brought bang up to date.

▼The 350Z draws inspiration from the 240Z of the 1960s, but updated for the 21st century

Like the original, the 350Z was front-engined, although Nissan preferred to call it 'front mid-ship'. In other words, the engine was located well-back under the bonnet to give near-perfect 53/47 weight distribution. The engine itself was an all-alloy 3.5-litre V8 unit that produced a useful 280bhp, going through a six-speed manual transmission to the back wheels. Performance figures were impressive, with a top speed of 155mph and a 0-60mph time of 5.9 seconds.

The suspension was race-car inspired, being an advanced multilink, fully independent system, with many of the components made of

aluminium to reduce unsprung weight. Braking, meanwhile, was courtesy of Brembo ABS- and EBD-equipped vented discs at each corner. Nissan's Vehicle Dynamic Control (VDC) stability control system was an option.

However, the 350Z was also a comfortable cruiser for two people, with a well-specified interior that included, unusually, a driver's seat which was shaped differently to the passenger's. and an instrument pod that moved in conjunction with the adjustable steering wheel.

The Nissan 350Z brought the legendary Z concept back to form and introduced it to a whole new generation of car enthusiasts.

▲ The 350Z's cockpit is a modern, comfortable place to be

SPECIFICATION

Capacity: 3498cc
Cylinders: V6
Compression ratio: 10.3:1
Maximum power: 280bhp at 6200rpm
Maximum torque: 362Nm at 4800rpm
Gearbox: Manual, six-speed
Length: 4310mm
Width: 1815mm
Weight: 1547kg
0-60mph: 5.9 seconds
Maximum speed: 155mph

Noble M400

2004 United Kingdom

HOW TO SPOT

Compact and curvaceous coupe with triple headlamps in scalloped recesses, large air intakes in rear wings, integral rear spoiler with additional wing above.

▼ The M400 has become a trackday favourite. And no wonder, with superb handling and performance

It's rare for a new supercar company to appear, and even rarer for one to succeed. But the first Noble was produced in 1998 and the company has gone from strength to strength, building world-beating performance cars.

The man behind the company, Lee Noble, had been building specialist cars since the 1980s, including the Ultima and Ascari sports cars. He was also an accomplished racing driver and engineer, so well placed to design his own cars.

That first Noble was badged M10 and was deemed a wonderful car to drive, but the styling of its open-top glassfibre body came in for criticism. Noble listened to the critics and responded

with the M12, which had essentially the same chassis as the previous car but in a restyled closed coupe that looked superb. The mid-engined M12's handling was beyond reproof, and the 310bhp output of the Ford V6 ensured sparkling performance in the lightweight body. Journalists were falling over themselves to give this bold newcomer awards as 'Best Driver's car'.

And then, in 2004, Noble wheeled out an even more powerful incarnation of the M12. The M400 uses the same basic chassis and body but has been treated to an uprated version of the 3.0-litre Ford engine.

SPECIFICATION

Capacity: 2968cc

Cylinders: V6

Compression ratio: 8.0:1

Maximum power: 425bhp at 6500rpm

Maximum torque: 529Nm at 5000rpm

Gearbox: Six-speed manual

Length: 4089mm

Width: 1885mm

Weight: 1160kg

0-60mph: 3.5 seconds

Maximum speed: 185mph

Twin turbochargers and internal modifications have increased the maximum power to 425bhp. In a car weighing just 1160kg, this ensures a staggering 0-60mph time of just 3.5 seconds, and a top speed of no less than 185mph.

Most Nobles are bought for track use, and that's just where the M400 is most at home. With no electronic driver aids, such as traction control, and all the power going to the back wheels only, this is a car that demands respect. That said, it is a remarkably civilised machine on the road, despite the no-frills interior.

The Noble M400 may not look like a perfect car, with its glassfibre bodyshell and muddled dash layout, but once you get behind the wheel and start driving the thing in anger, it becomes as near perfect as you could possibly wish.

▲ The M400's cockpit is simple and functional - what more do you need on a track?

Noble M14
2006 United Kingdom

Not content with producing some of the world's best-handling cars for track enthusiasts, Lee Noble went on to take on the likes of the Porsche 911 Turbo and Ferrari F430, with his M14 supercar. This was a car for people who demand luxury and performance.

The M14 used a new steel spaceframe chassis that drew upon the success of the Noble M400 to ensure unsurpassed handling capabilities. It was shod in a distinctive glassfibre body (a carbonfibre version could follow) that had hints of Porsche and Ferrari about it, and boasted

▼ From behind, the M14 looks menacing and powerful

an aggressiveness and presence that the M400 lacked.

Behind the seats sat a Ford-soured V6 engine with a capacity of 3.0-litres and this was fed by a pair of turbochargers to help create 400bhp of power that went, via a six-speed manual gearbox, to the back wheels. It was enough to give true supercar performance, with a top speed of 190mph and a 0-60mph time of 4.3 seconds, while at the same giving enough tractability to be easy to drive in traffic.

Previous Nobles were criticised by the quality of their interiors – something that was of no real consequence to track enthusiasts. For the M14 market, though, a luxurious cockpit was demanded, so Noble went all out to create just that. The seats were specially made with carbonfibre frames and covered with high-quality Italian leather (as used by Ferrari). The same leather could also be found on the door panels and dashboard. All the instruments and

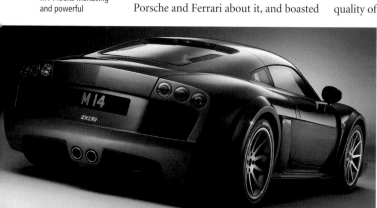

▲ The M14 takes Noble into true supercar territory

SPECIFICATION

Capacity: 2968cc
Cylinders: V6
Compression ratio: 8.5:1
Maximum power: 400bhp at 6100rpm
Maximum torque: 522Nm at 4750rpm
Gearbox: Six-speed manual
Length: 4267mm
Width: 1935mm
Weight: 1100kg
0-60mph: 4.3 seconds
Maximum speed: 190mph

controls were easy to use, with some of the most frequently required buttons being located on the steering wheel itself.

The M14 was also practical, with plenty of room for two people to sit in comfort, and a decent amount of luggage space in compartments at the front and rear of the car.

Noble, with its stunning M14, is single-handedly reinventing the British supercar industry. And that can only be a good thing. This is a company with a very exciting future ahead of it.

Pagani Zonda C12 F

2005 Italy

The Pagani Zonda C12 first appeared in 1999 and was the brainchild of Argentinean-born Horacio Pagani, who had previously worked at Lamborghini in Italy before setting up his own engineering company in that country.

The Zonda was a striking car with lines inspired – we're told – by the curves of Mrs Pagani's body! The beautifully shaped car, with its taut lines, simply oozes power and is hand-built from lightweight carbonfibre. The shape is designed – not only to look good – but also to push the car down onto the road at high speeds to ensure stability.

The Zonda C12 F first appeared in 2005, and the suffix stood for Fangio – Pagani was close friends with the legendary racing driver, who helped

▼ The Zonda looks as if it's just landed from another planet!

Stunning two-seater coupe with thrust-forward cabin. Very curvaceous front wings with six protruding projector headlamps. Long rear deck with separate spoiler. Four exhaust tailpipes grouped together in central outlet.

with the design of the car. The F was a development of the original C12 and was lighter in weight and had a more powerful engine – in short, it was an even faster car.

Hidden under that long rear deck was a 7.3-litre V12 Mercedes-Benz engine that was a work of art in itself to look at. The engine produced 620bhp – 70bhp more than the standard Zonda C12 – which gave the supercar a top speed of 214mph, while it could reach 60mph in just 3.6 seconds.

Inside, the Zonda F was even more striking. There was hardly any plastic to be seen; just leather, aluminium, wood and carbonfibre, all lovingly hand-crafted to create one of the most incredible cockpits ever. Especially wonderful were the alloy dials which hada retro look about them.

The Zonda C12 F was also available in Clubsport form, which was even lighter and faster, with a 650bhp engine. This version of the car had an incredible power-to-weight ratio of 521bhp/ton.

Pagani invested in a new factory in the early 21st Century to increase production of the Zonda from around 25 cars a year to 250. It will be on sale in the USA for the first time from 2007. Even these figures are tiny on a worldwide scale, though, so ownership of a Pagani Zonda will remain very exclusive.

▲ Inside, the Pagani appears to have come from the past, with a bizarre but endearing retro look

SPECIFICATION

Capacity: 7291cc
Cylinders: V12
Compression ratio: n/a
Maximum power: 620bhp at 6150rpm
Maximum torque: 400Nm at 4000rpm
Gearbox: Six-speed manual
Length: 4435mm
Width: 2055mm
Weight: 1234kg
0-60mph: 3.6 seconds
Maximum speed: 214mph

Panoz Esperante

2001 United States

HOW TO SPOT

Sleek open-topped two seater with long bulging bonnet, swept-back headlamps and straked vents in front wings.

At first sight, you'd be mistaken for thinking that the Esperante was a traditional, low-volume British sports car, with its long bonnet and understated looks. However, it was designed and built in the USA, by one of the country's only low-volume car manufacturers – Panoz.

The Esperante was the brainchild of

▼ The Esperante looks more European than American

Daniel Panez, who started his company in 1989 and went on to become well-known for his involvement in US motorsport, in particular ALMS.

The Panez Esperante first appeared in 2001 and was more hi-tech than its looks suggested, with a bonded aluminium chassis under aluminium

and carbonfibre body panels to keep the weight down. Although the Esperante had a folding roof, there was also a GT version with a sleek fixed lid.

The engine was front-mounted, but positioned well back to give a good front to rear weight distribution. It was a 4.6-litre Ford V8 all-alloy unit with four valves per cylinder that produced 320bhp, which led through a five-speed gearbox to the rear wheels.

Inside, the Esperante had a luxurious feel, with plenty of hand-finished leather and wood covering the seats and dash areas. Unusually, the instrument pod was mounted in the centre of the dashboard, instead of in front of the driver.

The Esperante offered lively performance, with a 0-60mph time of 5.1 seconds and a top speed of 155mph. However, Panoz developed a faster version in the form of the GTLM, which boasted a supercharged engine that developed 420bhp and rocketed the car to 60mph in 4.2 seconds and on to 180mph. Beyond that, there was also the GTS racecar which had lightweight plastic panels and a 5.8-litre, 430bhp engine. The GTS proved popular as an affordable racecar and was also adopted by some US racing schools.

The Panoz Esperante offered discerning American buyers a unique and exciting alternative to similarly priced sports cars from larger manufacturers on both sides of the Atlantic.

▲ The leather-trimmed cockpit is unusual in that the instruments are mounted centrally

SPECIFICATION

Capacity: 4601cc
Cylinders: V8
Compression ratio: 9.8:1
Maximum power: 320bhp at 6000rpm
Maximum torque: 430Nm at 4750rpm
Gearbox: Manual, five-speed
Length: 4478mm
Width: 1859mm
Weight: 1451kg
0-60mph: 5.1 seconds
Maximum speed: 155mph

Porsche 911 Carrera 2.7 RS

1973 Germany

Today, the Carrera 2.7 RS is, quite simply, the most sought-after production 911 ever. It's reached almost legendary status among Porsche aficionados, and prices are sky-high.

Yet this oh-so-perfect sports car almost never happened. The RS was developed as a homologation special to allow Porsche to compete in GT racing – the company was required to build 500 road-going cars in order to qualify. However, the marketing department doubted whether they could persuade

▼ The 2.7RS is one of the most sought-after Porsches ever built

people to pay a premium for a 911 with few creature comforts. Thankfully, they were overruled.

The car was developed from the 911S but was significantly modified to improve performance. The 2.4S engine was increased in capacity to 2681cc to push power to 210bhp at 6300rpm and torque to 255Nm at 5100rpm – a useful increase over the 911S's 190bhp.

However, the main performance gains were made by putting the car on a weight-saving programme. The roof, wings and

HOW TO SPOT

Classic 911 body-shape, often with bold 'Carrera' side decals and colour-coded wheels. 'Ducktail' rear spoiler with 'Carrera RS' and '2.7' badging.

bonnet were made of thinner (and so lighter) steel, while the windscreen and rear quarter windows used thinner glass.

The rear arches were flared to accommodate wider Fuchs alloy wheels, and there was the option (which most buyers took) of a distinctive 'ducktail' spoiler to give added downforce.

Also optional were large and distinctive 'Carrera' side stripes that ran from the front to rear arches. Offered in red, blue, black or green, you could have the Fuchs wheel centres colour-coded to match. Combined with distinctive Grand Prix White paintwork, this gave what is now recognised as the classic, and much imitated, RS look.

The Carrera RS was produced in two road-going versions. The RS Sport (often called Lightweight) had a very basic specification to keep the weight down to just 975kg. However, not everyone wanted to rough it, which is why Porsche also made the more popular RS Touring model, with a fully specced interior.

A total of 1580 RS cars were built. Of these, the majority were Tourings and 200 were Sports. There were also

17 in the very basic RSH homologation specification, and 55 were race-ready RSRs. The latter boasted a rollcage, even wider rear arches and a 2.8-litre engine that produced 300bhp.

Today the Carrera RS is the Holy Grail of Porsches, and good genuine ones are extremely sought-after, leading to a healthy business in replicas, based on contemporary 911s.

The rear of the RS is defined by the classic ducktail spoiler

SPECIFICATION

Capacity: 2687cc
Cylinders: flat-six
Compression ratio: 8.5:1
Maximum power: 210bhp at 6300rpm
Maximum torque: 255Nm at 5100rpm
Gearbox: Manual, five-speed
Length: 4163mm
Width: 1610mm
Weight: 1975kg (Sport)
0-60mph: 5.6 seconds
Maximum speed: 153mph

Porsche 911 Turbo

1975 Germany

HOW TO SPOT

Distinctive 911 body shape endowed with wide front and rear arches, massive 'teat-ray' rear spoiler, and full-width rear reflector announcing the word 'Porsche'

In 1974, Porsche announced a car that would take the motoring world by storm and go on to become a legend in its own right.

That car was the 911 Turbo and, bizarre as it seems today, was originally planned as a limited-edition run of 500 cars with a stripped out, race-inspired interior. Thankfully, though, interest was so great that Porsche decided to build the car as an on-going, luxury model at the top of the 911 range.

Mounted at the back of the new Porsche was a 2994cc flat-six engine with a secret weapon – a single KKK turbocharger which was powered by the exhaust gases from both cylinder banks. Spinning at up to 100,000rpm, the turbo helped create a maximum power output of 260bhp at 5500rpm – an astonishing amount

▼The Turbo had wider front and rear wings than the standard 911. This is a 1975 car

▲ The rear of the early Turbo had the trademark whaletail spoiler

in the mid-1970s when turbocharged road-going cars were still a novelty. By comparison, the standard 911 Carrera 3.0 of the day produced 200bhp.

The bodyshell was based on that of the contemporary 911 but fitted with much-extended wheel arches front and rear that gave the Turbo its distinctive aggressive appearance. The whaletail rear spoiler may have debuted on the earlier 911 3.0 RS, but it soon became inextricably linked to the 911 Turbo.

Surprisingly, perhaps, the 911 Turbo was equipped with a four-speed gearbox – Porsche claimed that the five-gear 915 unit used in the standard 911 wouldn't cope with the extra power and, besides,

SPECIFICATION

Capacity: 2994cc

Cylinders: flat-six

Compression ratio: 6.5:1

Maximum power: 260bhp at 5500rpm

Maximum torque: 343Nm at 4000rpm

Gearbox: Four-speed manual

Length: 4491mm

Width: 1775mm

Weight: 1195kg

0-60mph: 6.4 sec

Maximum speed: 152mph

the engine's power and torque were such that four gears were all that were required.

To fill those massive arches, the Turbo was equipped with 15-inch Fuchs alloy wheels, which were 7-inches wide at the front and 8-inches wide at the rear.

The 911 Turbo developed steadily over the years, gaining more power as it went along. In 1993 it gained four-wheel-drive and a twin-turbocharged 3.6-litre engine that produced a healthy 408bhp. In 2000 it was replaced by an all-new version with a watercooled engine.

It may have seemed mad producing a gas-guzzling supercar in the middle of the 1970s' fuel shortages, but it paid off and the 911 Turbo was a great success, and went on to become a motoring legend in its own right. It's become the definitive Porsche, its distinctive shape has graced many a poster and its always been the car that other manufacturers have used as a benchmark.

Porsche 924 Carrera GT

1980 Germany

▲ Wider arches and a massive bonnet scoop gave the GT an aggressive edge over the standard 924

The 924 was Porsche's entry-level car, introduced in 1976. Its smooth lines and practical two-plus-two hatchback configuration made it a great sales success, but the lacklustre performance from the 2-litre, 125bhp engine was never going to set the world on fire.

That, though, was all to change in 1980 when Porsche put the 924 on steroids and unveiled the mad 924 Carrera GT. Designed as an homologation special for the FISA Group 3 production sports car

class, just 400 were built, with 75 right-hand-drive examples coming to the UK.

The 2-litre engine was developed from the 924 Turbo, and a larger turbocharger plus other enhancements pushed the power output to 210bhp – no one could accuse this 924 of being underpowered. The transmission, suspension and brakes were all uprated to cope with the increased power.

All this, though, was overshadowed by what Porsche did to the 924's delicate and

HOW TO SPOT

Stylish 924 two-door hatchback coupe, enhanced with 'stuck on' front and rear arch extensions. Pop-up headlamps with four small air intakes between. Large bonnet scoop.

▲ The GT's rear arches were stuck-on plastic items

smooth lines. Polyurethane front and rear wheel arch extensions suddenly gave the petite 924 an aggressive and businesslike appearance. An impression that was enhanced by air intakes in the nose plus a massive bonnet scoop; the latter accommodating the turbo's intercooler. However you looked at it, there was no doubt that the 924 Carrera GT meant business.

The GT was available only in black, red or silver, while the interiors were all black with red-pinstripe fabric on the seat centres.

Driving the Carrera GT took some getting used to. The big turbocharger took time to spool up, so there was a distinct lag between pressing the accelerator and something happening. But when it finally happened, you knew about it!

Porsche went on to produce the Carrera GTS in 1981, which was even more extreme. Glassfibre body panels and a lack of sound insulation made it a full 60kg lighter than the GT. That, combined with a power output of 245bhp, made the GTS a seriously fast car, reaching 60mph

in 6.2 seconds and going on to a top speed of 155mph. It can be distinguished from the GT by its fixed, recessed headlamps.

The 924 Carrera GT is a rare car, but its styling went on to be the inspiration for the mainstream 944 which replaced the 924. This had the same bulging wheel arches, albeit better integrated with the surrounding bodywork.

SPECIFICATION

Capacity: 1984cc
Cylinders: straight-four
Compression ratio: 8.5:1
Maximum power: 210bhp at 6000rpm
Maximum torque: 280Nm at 3500rpm
Gearbox: Five-speed manual
Length: 4212mm
Width: 1755mm
Weight: 1180kg
0-60mph: 6.7 sec
Maximum speed: 150mph

Porsche 959

1986 Germany

HOW TO SPOT

Sleek two-plus-two bodyshell with swept-back headlamps, flared wheel-arches with air vents in the rears, and large rear spoiler.

Developed as an homologation special to enable Porsche to compete in Gruppe B motorsport, the 959 was one of the most technologically advanced – and fastest – cars ever built.

Based on a 911, the 959 had carbonfibre body panels, sophisticated four-wheel-drive, six-speed gearbox, active suspension, magnesium-alloy wheels with tyre-pressure sensors, run-flat tyres, and stunningly styled lines.

At the rear of the car was a twin turbocharged engine. This was a four-valve per cylinder, hybrid air- and water-cooled unit based on the 2.65-litre engine developed for the 956 and 962 race cars. For the 959, the capacity was increased to 2.85-litres.

The sequential twin-turbocharger system was developed to overcome, to a large extent, the marked turbo-lag that was a characteristic of the 911 Turbo of the day. At low revs all the exhaust gases powered the right-hand turbocharger to give a light boost. Once the revs started to climb the left-hand blower started to kick in, powered by that side's exhaust, to give the full 450bhp. So you still got a distinct turbo 'kick' but not at the expense of low-speed driveability.

But perhaps the greatest innovation of the 959 was its drivetrain. It was the first ever Porsche – not to mention the first true sports car – to feature four-wheel-drive. Power from the rear-mounted engine went through a six-speed gearbox with a transaxle driving the rear wheels, while a propshaft led forward to a second differential driving the front wheels. The power split between the front and rear axles was varied, either automatically or manually, to suit the driving conditions.

▼ The 959 still looks modern today

The 959's lines were positively space age compared to the standard 911

The suspension, too, could be adjusted in height and firmness, so that the car sat lower at high-speeds, or with increased ground clearance for negotiating rough surfaces.

SPECIFICATION

Capacity: 2847cc

Cylinders: flat-six

Compression ratio: 8.3:1

Maximum power: 450bhp at 6500rpm

Maximum torque: 500Nm at 5500rpm

Gearbox: Manual, six-speed

Length: 4260mm

Width: 1840mm

Weight: 1650kg

0-60mph: 3.6 seconds

Maximum speed: 197mph

All this technology was clad in a body based on the galvanised-steel shell of the contemporary 911 Turbo. However, the doors and front luggage-compartment lid were lightweight aluminium, while most of the remaining panels are made from Kevlar and carbonfibre.

Two specifications were offered, and the vast majority of cars were built to what Porsche called Confort (yes, that's the correct spelling) specification. A handful were Sport models that were stripped of variable ride height, central-locking, electric windows and seats, air-conditioning and a passenger-side door mirror, to save 100kg in weight.

It is believed that just 292 road-going 959s were built, making it a rare and sought-after machine.

Porsche 928 GTS

1992 Germany

HOW TO SPOT

Large, very rounded two-door coupe with extended wheel arches, exposed pop-up headlamps and full-width rear reflector.

The Porsche 928 dates right back to 1978 and it was developed to replace the legendary 911, but it never did. It was a quite different car, with a large, water-cooled V8 engine mounted at the front, driving the back wheels via a rear-mounted gearbox, to give an even weight distribution.

The 928 was a large car and boasted spaceship-like lines that seemed very futuristic in the mid-1970s, with exposed pop-up headlamps and lots of glass, including a lifting hatchback to give access to the luggage area.

It was the same story inside, with a luxurious and modern interior that boasted an instrument pod that moved in conjunction with the steering column. The back seats cocooned small children in comfort, while in the front there was

▼ The GTS was the ultimate incarnation of the 928 and still looks modern today

plenty of space for two adults to stretch out and enjoy long journeys.

Over the years, the 928 evolved into the last and best version – the GTS of 1992. This had a 5.3-litre, 32-valve V8 engine that produced 350bhp (by contrast, the first 928 had 240bhp). With a 0-60mph time of 5.6 seconds and a top speed of 171mph, this truly was a supercar. Also, unlike most earlier 928s, the GTS had a five-speed manual gearbox, not an automatic, to make the best use of the power, while the suspension was firmer to improve the handling.

The GTS also had restyled bodywork that dragged the 928 into the 1990s and

gave it a more aggressive appearance. The wings bulged purposefully to accommodate wider wheels, the front and rear ends were updated with smoother lines and, at the rear was a large, body-coloured spoiler in place of the earlier cars' rubber item.

The interior was fundamentally unchanged from that of earlier 928s, but was treated to full leather trim and equipment updates to ensure it still looked modern. It was a wonderful place in which to be transported in speed and style across continents.

The 928 was quietly discontinued in 1995, while the 911 – which it was meant to replace – has gone from strength to strength. However, the 928 – especially in GTS guise – was a great car in its own right, and its space-age lines still look modern today. There aren't many cars from the 1970s you can say that about!

The 928 had a front-mounted V8 engine linked to a gearbox at the rear for perfect weight distribution

SPECIFICATION

Capacity: 5397cc

Cylinders: V8

Compression ratio: 10.4:1

Maximum power: 350bhp at 5700rpm

Maximum torque: 491Nm at 4250rpm

Gearbox: Five-speed manual

Length: 4519mm

Width: 1849mm

Weight: 1600kg

0-60mph: 5.6 seconds

Maximum speed: 171mph

Porsche 911 Turbo S
2004 Germany

The Turbo S was available in Cabriolet form for the ultimate in open-top motoring

By the start of the 21st century, the 911 Turbo had developed into what many regarded as the best sports car in the world. It's power, handling, practicality and durability were all hard to beat. Four-wheel-drive and electronic driver aids had tamed the older Turbo's sometimes wayward handling, while a twin-turbocharged, water-cooled engine – still mounted at the back – gave almost seamless power delivery, with only a hint of the old turbo lag.

However, in 2004, Porsche produced an even better version – the 911 Turbo S. This last of the 996-model Turbos had an output of 450bhp, thanks to a 30bhp power upgrade that had previously been offered as an option to buyers of the standard Turbo. The upgrade consisted of larger KKK turbochargers, uprated intercoolers and a revised engine management system. As well as the extra power (which peaked at just 5700rpm), the torque was increased from 560Nm to no less than 620Nm, which was available from 3500 to 4500rpm.

Wide rear arches with large air intakes in each side, three massive front air intakes, fixed rear spoiler with extendable section.

To keep this power in check, the Turbo S was fitted with Porsche's ceramic brake discs. Made from carbon-reinforced silicon carbide, these were gripped by six-piston calipers that had a distinctive yellow finish. The advantage of these brakes, said Porsche, was that they were lighter, more responsive, performed better in the wet and would last for over 150,000 miles.

Visually, the Turbo S was identical to the standard 911 Turbo, but the 18-inch alloys were finished in GT Metallic Silver – a shade that was used on the bodywork of the Carrera GT supercar – with coloured Porsche crests in the centres.

Inside, there were one or two more changes. The 'Turbo S' logo appeared on the door sills, centre console tachometer. The instruments themselves had a unique aluminium finish, while the leather of the seat centres, steering wheel rim, gearlever and handbrake lever have a special embossed finish. Standard equipment for the Turbo S included sat-nav, six-CD changer and cruise control.

In creating the Turbo S, Porsche proved that even it could make the best even better.

▲From behind you can see the Turbo's wider rear arches and fixed rear spoiler

SPECIFICATION

Capacity: 3600cc
Cylinders: flat-six
Compression ratio: 9.4:1
Maximum power: 450bhp at 5000rpm
Maximum torque: 620Nm at 3500 to 4400rpm
Gearbox: Six-speed manual or optional Tiptronic
Length: 4435mm
Width: 1830mm
Weight: 1590kg (coupé)
0-60mph: 4.0 seconds
Maximum speed: 191mph

Porsche Carrera GT

2003 Germany

When Porsche decided to produce a range-topping supercar, it didn't hold back. The exciting Carrera GT was, in many ways, a road-going race car that utilised space-age technology.

▼The Carrera GT is unmistakeably a Porsche, albeit a very special one

For instance, it was the world's first production car to use a carbon-reinforced plastic chassis. This offered a substantial weight-saving over metal, while much of the car's bodywork was also lightweight carbonfibre and Kevlar; as were the seats. All this meant that the Carrera GT weighed in at just 1380kg.

Saving weight means better performance, which is extra-good news when you consider that the GT's mid-mounted V10 engine produced 610bhp – a fact which is even more impressive when you learn that it was a normally aspirated (in other words, not turbocharged or supercharged).

That power drove the rear wheels only (to enhance the race-car feel) via a six-speed gearbox and – another world first – a ceramic clutch. This remarkable innovation was lightweight and only 169mm in diameter, yet could more than cope with the phenomenal

Sleek two-seater, mid-engined roadster
with projector headlamps, massive side
air-intakes, twin humps behind the seats,
with V10 engine visible under.

▲ The mid-
mounted engine
sits under those
twin humps

forces involved; and it would outlast a
conventional clutch.

The massive 340mm brake discs were
also ceramic, rather than steel, which
meant they could better cope with high
temperatures and, again, were lighter and
longer-lasting than conventional discs.

The Carrera GT had a relatively simple,
two-seat, carbonfibre-trimmed cockpit
which reflected its racing pedigree.
Indeed, the birch-wood gearknob harked
back to the golden days of motorsport.
The driving position was perfect, with the
gearstick and other controls all close at
hand, while the leather-clad bucket seats
offered excellent support during high-
speed cornering.

Although an open-top car, the Carrera
GT came with a Targa-type roof system
comprising of a pair of lightweight
carbonfibre shells, which could be stored
in the luggage compartment when not
in use.

The shape of the Carrera GT was
stunning, but it was also functional.
Like a race car, it was designed to create
downforce to hold the car onto the
road at high speed. At its maximum

speed of 205mph, the GT developed a
downforce of 4000 Newtons, which was
the equivalent of a load of 400kg pushing
down on the rear axle. Furthermore, the
car's carbonfibre undertrays created a
suction effect that further helped to hold
it onto the road.

SPECIFICATION

Capacity: 5.7-litre
Cylinders: V10
Compression ratio: 12.0:1
Maximum power: 612bhp at 8000rpm
Maximum torque: 590Nm at 5750rpm
Gearbox: Manual, six-speed
Length: 4610mm
Width: 1920mm
Weight: 1380kg
0-60mph: 3.6 seconds
Maximum speed: 205mph

Subaru Impreza WRX STi

1993 Japan

The Subaru Impreza WRX became the performance car of choice for a generation. And for good reason, too; it won the World Rally Championship three years running in 1996, 1996 and 1997; thanks in no small part to the driving abilities of Colin McRae and the late Richard Burns. Skills which millions have tried to emulate on exciting computer games featuring the Impreza.

It's this heritage that's made the Impreza, especially in WRX form, such an icon; plus its astonishing performance and value for money. Its success was

▼ The Impreza may not be pretty, but it certainly looks as if it means business

HOW TO SPOT

Mid-sized four-door saloon with prominent wheelarch extensions, large bonnet scoop and massive rear spoiler. Gold-finished alloy wheels.

certainly not down to its looks; a more unlikely-looking sports car there has never been. Essentially a boxy four-door saloon, the Impreza was endowed with big wheel arches, bonnet scoop and prominent rear wing, just like the rally car. And a trademark feature was gold-painted wheels. Subtle it was not.

The performance was far from subtle, either. Powered by a turbocharged, flat-four (essentially the same configuration as an old VW Beetle) 2.0-litre engine, the WRX (in 2005 form) had 265bhp on tap. The unusual engine configuration ensured a low centre of gravity which, in part, was responsible for the car's excellent handling; both on the road and on the rally track.

The power was fed to all four wheels to ensure optimum traction and handling, so 60mph was reached in a mere 5.5 seconds, and the WRX went on to a top speed of 152mph. Not bad for a four-seater saloon costing around £25,000, and coming from a company that was better known for its staid four-wheel-drive estate cars!

The Subaru rally cars were prepared by UK-based Prodrive and, over the years,

this motorsport company has given its name to some limited-edition road-going Imprezas. These had more powerful engines, revised suspension and brakes, modified bodywork and interiors, and special badging.

The original Impreza was replaced by a revised model in 2000, but has remained essentially the same car throughout its life, retaining the original mechanical configuration and boy-racer looks. After all, that is the appeal of the WRX.

▲ Gold wheels and a massive rear spoiler are Impreza trademarks

SPECIFICATION

Capacity: 1994cc
Cylinders: Flat-four
Compression ratio: 8.0:1
Maximum power: 265bhp at 6000rpm
Maximum torque: 343Nm at 4000rpm
Gearbox: Six-speed manual
Length: 4415mm
Width: 1740mm
Weight: 1475
0-60mph: 5.5 seconds
Maximum speed: 152mph

TVR Cerbera Speed 12

1999 United Kingdom

It's not often that a manufacturer develops a car and then decides not to sell it to the public because it's just too powerful. Yet that is what happened with the TVR Cerbera Speed 12. Company boss, Peter Wheeler, wanted to produce a car that would beat the McLaren F1. And, while the F1 relied on high-technology, the Speed 12 drew on good old-fashioned brute power.

And what power it was! The TVR-developed V12 engine (basically two V6 units joined together) had a capacity of 7.7-litres and produced no less than 800bhp without the aid of turbochargers or superchargers. The engine was linked to a six-speed manual gearbox driving the rear wheels. Legend had it that the

The Speed 12 looks outrageous from any angle. Look at those side-mounted exhausts

HOW TO SPOT

Low and wide curvaceous coupe with four angled projector headlamps, large sill extensions, jutting out rear bumper and large rear spoiler.

unit broke a dynometer during testing because it was so powerful.

Despite the stupendous power, TVR still ensured that the Speed 12 was extremely light in weight. A carbonfibre bodyshell sat atop tubular-steel and aluminium honeycomb chassis and the entire car weighed just over 1000kg.

In true TVR tradition, the body looked as outrageous as the car's specification, with long, low and wide lines, and a chopped roofline that gave the Speed 12 a mean and aggressive appearance. Inside was a different story, though, with the cockpit being simple and austere, like a racecar, in an effort to keep the weight down.

A handful of race-ready Speed 12s were built and tested on track. TVR claimed that the car could reach speeds of around 240mph and would hit 60mph in just 3.2 seconds. Figures that put the Blackpool beast on a par with the legendary McLaren F1.

Orders were taken for the £160,000 machine but, after Peter Wheeler drove it, he decided that 800bhp in such a lightweight car was simply too dangerous

and the programme was cancelled. However, one lucky customer in the UK did, in fact, buy a road-going Speed 12, and this has made guest appearances at supercar events around the country.

As it is, though, the TVR Cerbera Speed 12 remains one of the greatest supercars never to be put into production.

The Speed 12's interior is not as slick as the outside, but is stripped right down to keep weight to a minimum

SPECIFICATION

Capacity: 7736cc
Cylinders: V12
Compression ratio: 12.5:1
Maximum power: 800bhp at 7250rpm
Maximum torque: 881Nm at 5750rpm
Gearbox: Manual, six-speed
Length: n/a
Width: n/a
Weight: 1070kg
0-60mph: 3.2 seconds
Maximum speed: 240mph

Ultima GTR

1999 United Kingdom

HOW TO SPOT

Two-seater coupe with very low front end between bulging wings. Bulbous cabin with curved windscreen and roof-mounted air intake. Large rear spoiler.

▼ The Ultima is one of the fastest cars around – and it looks it!

In 2005, what was essentially A kit car broke the world record for the fastest accelerating car, reaching 60mph in just 2.7 seconds. It also set a new record in reaching 100mph in an incredible 5.8 seconds. And then went on to break a third record by accelerating from standstill to 100mph and then braking back to standstill in 9.8 seconds. These figures were better than anything achieved by such exotica as the Ferrari Enzo and McLaren F1.

The Ultima story dates back to 1983 when Lee Noble (later to produce the Noble cars) built the Ultima MkI with a mid-mounted Ford V6 engine and looks based on a Le Mans racecar. Over the years, the component car developed and a Chevrolet V8 engine became a popular power source. Interestingly, in 1991 McLaren bought two Ultima MkII kits to use in the development of its F1 supercar. A year later, Lee Noble sold the company to one of his customers, but the Ultima continued to be developed, resulting in the GTR which first appeared in 1999.

The all-new GTR took build quality to new levels and featured a lightweight tubular-steel spaceframe chassis with

▲The Ultima exposed! No wonder the car is so light – there's really not much to it

integral rollcage. Over this went the unstressed glassfibre bodyshell with its compact and distinctive racecar styling. The mid-mounted engine was a specially built Chevrolet V8 unit linked to a Porsche gearbox and transaxle, driving the rear wheels. Power depended on what you specified, but could be as much as 534bhp which, combined with a body that weighed less than 1000kg, accounted for the phenomenal acceleration. The fully independent suspension was racecar-developed, with double unequal-length wishbones and fully adjustable dampers.

As always, the Ultima was offered either as a complete, ready to drive car, or in component form for self-build. Fully built, it was about the same price as a standard Porsche 911; but with the performance of a car costing much more. Build it yourself and you ended up with the same performance for even less money. How satisfying would that be?

SPECIFICATION

Capacity: 6300cc
Cylinders: V8
Compression ratio: n/a
Maximum power: 534bhp
Maximum torque: 716Nm
Gearbox: Five-speed manual
Length: 4000mm
Width: 1850mm
Weight: 990kg
0-60mph: 2.7 seconds
Maximum speed: 231mph

Vector WX-3

1992 United States

HOW TO SPOT

Wide and low mid-engined coupe with narrow nose, very deep sills, large side air intakes and long rear deck with louvres over.

The Vector car company never quite made it, despite the best efforts of company boss, Gerald Wiegart. The American built his first Vector, the W2, in 1978 as a concept car which late went into (very) limited production in the early 1980s. In 1991 the mid-engined supercar evolved into the W8, which was a 200mph-plus machine powered by a 600bhp V8 engine. Just

▼ The Vector WX-3 was a striking car which, sadly, was doomed to failure

17 examples were sold.

This was replaced by the WX-3, which was Wiegert's dream car. Based on the W8, it was powered by the same Chevrolet V8 engine, driving the rear wheels through an automatic gearbox. The turbocharged unit produced 600bhp of power, and Weigert claimed that his car was capable of 250mph.

The striking bodywork was made of

lightweight Kevlar and carbonfibre, and was mounted on a tubular steel and aluminium chassis with integral rollcage.

Inside, the WX-3's cockpit was more like that of an aircraft than a car. The instrumentation was all electronic and the driver was faced with an impressive mass of controls. Unusually, the car seated three people in a row.

In 1993, Vector was bought out by an Indonesian company called Megatech which, at the time, also owned Lamborghini. Weigert was offered a position as a designer, but turned it down and retained the rights to the W8 and WX-3 cars, which meant that the latter never went into production.

▲ The WX-3 had a hi-tech dashboard and was very modern for its time

SPECIFICATION

Capacity: 5998cc

Cylinders: V8

Compression ratio: n/a

Maximum power: 600bhp at 5700rpm

Maximum torque: 813Nm at 4900rpm

Gearbox: Automatic, three-speed

Length: 4368mm

Width: 1930mm

Weight: 1620kg

0-60mph: 3.3 seconds

Maximum speed: 250mph

Under Megatech's control, Vector produced the M12, which was an evolution of the WX-3 but powered by a Lamborghini engine and developed in Europe. Only 14 cars were built before the company ran into financial difficulties. Later, a similar car was built and powered by an American Corvette engine. This was called the SRV8 but, again, never made it into production.

Gerald Weigert regained control of the Vector name but, to date, no more cars have been built. Which is a shame because the concept cars, although flawed, showed great potential and, if nothing else, were exciting machines to behold.

The pictures in this book were provided courtesy of the following:

COVER IMAGE COURTESY OF YAMAHA MOTOR UK LTD

MOTORING PICTURE LIBRARY, NATIONAL MOTOR MUSEUM
NEILL BRUCE'S AUTOMOBILE PHOTOLIBRARY
ASTON MARTIN
AUDI
BENTLEY
BMW
BUGATTI
CATERHAM
JAGUAR
LOTUS
MARCUS
MERCEDES
MG ROVER
NISSAN
NOBLE
PAGINI
PANOZ
PORSCHE
ULTIMA